*Wendy*

# 111 Museums in New York That You Must Not Miss

*Photographs by Ed Lefkowicz*

111

emons:

For Bill: My companion in museums and in life.

© Emons Verlag GmbH
All rights reserved
Photographs by Ed Lefkowicz, except see page 238
© Cover motif: shutterstock.com/Flas100; shutterstock.com/anna42f
Layout: Eva Kraskes, based on a design
by Lübbeke | Naumann | Thoben
Edited by Karen E. Seiger
Maps: altancicek.design, www.altancicek.de
Basic cartographical information from Openstreetmap,
© OpenStreetMap-Mitwirkende, ODbL
Printing and binding: Lensing Druck GmbH & Co. KG,
Feldbachacker 16, 44149 Dortmund
Printed in Germany 2018
ISBN 978-3-7408-0379-7
First edition

Did you enjoy this book? Do you want more?
Join us in uncovering new places around the world at:
www.111places.com

# Foreword

New Yorkers love their museums. It's an obsession. From the Frick to Folk Art, New York City has arguably the richest museum culture in the world. Exploring museums is a kind of urban sport – a personal quest to seek out the crème de la crème. And I could not agree more.

Museums are my happy places. As a private museum guide in New York City, I've spent countless hours at the Met, MoMA, and the Guggenheim. They never fail to inspire. But I've always wondered about all the other museums out there – the hidden ones waiting to be discovered.

With this guidebook, I challenged myself to visit 111 museums across the five boroughs in less than a year. It turned out to be the adventure of a lifetime. I trekked through basements and backroom ateliers from Brooklyn to Queens. I wandered through SoHo lofts and genteel private clubs. I learned about everything from Houdini to holograms, baseball to bonsai. Only here could a run-down apartment building be transformed into the beloved Tenement Museum. The journey was extraordinary.

Consider this book your personal museum concierge, a treasure map to the secret corners of the iconic museums, and a field guide to the kinds of museums you never dreamed existed. So, in addition to the classic institutions, you will find hidden exhibitions out there and tiny, one-room galleries filled with art, objects, and ideas. These are the places, big and small, that contain the repositories for our shared humanity.

You'll go inside a gallery filled with outsider art and discover the micro museum tucked in an alleyway. From the Noguchi Museum to Neue Galerie; fashion and food; miniatures, math, and modern art, New York City's museum culture is vast, vibrant, and original.

Museums connect us to the bigger world around us. And isn't that what being a New Yorker is all about?

– WL

# 111 Museums

# 1 101 Spring Street

*Order as art in life and work*

Iconic sculptor Donald Judd (1928–1994) preferred symmetry. Perhaps the best way to understand his repeating, rectilinear works is to visit his home and work space at 101 Spring Street. The artist worked and lived with his wife and two children in the five-story, 19th-century, cast-iron building in SoHo in the 1970s. Maintained by the Judd Foundation, this historic studio takes you on a journey into the creative world. It is a visual time capsule of 1970s New York.

Take a guided tour, and you'll see all the floors are laid out just as Judd left them. The light here is exceptional, with plentiful windows looking out on the cobblestone streets. Each level had a function, but it's the second-floor kitchen that is the most revealing, with its exact arrangement of open shelves of glasses, stacked plates and platters, knives, cutting boards, and even a rotary phone with its original number on the dial. It's the way Judd purposely placed these everyday objects that is so intriguing – an unwavering ordering of space. Just like his art.

Even though Judd is considered a pioneer of minimalism, he didn't like the term. The movement's idea was to take human emotion out of art and emphasize the object itself. Judd often used machine-made materials like steel to create his sculptures – not just the objects, but the space around them too. In the fifth-floor bedroom, Judd installed a platform bed on the ground. It offers uninterrupted views of the art all around, where works by friends of the sculptor, like John Chamberlain and Claes Oldenburg, are just as Judd placed them. The focal point is the 1970 Dan Flavin red and white fluorescent sculpture, which commands attention. Running the length of the room, the work's flickering light frames the night sky. It magically floats in the room and grounds it all at once. Perfectly placed by the artist, this work in this space is pure Judd.

Address 101 Spring Street, New York, NY 10012, +1 (212)219-2747, www.juddfoundation.org, info@juddfoundation.org | Getting there Subway to Spring Street (C, E, 6), Prince Street (N, R), Broadway/Lafayette Street (M) | Hours See website to arrange a guided visit | Tip Some of the city's best films and documentaries are shown at the nearby Film Forum, a beloved art-house mainstay since 1970, with foreign films, independents, and American classics (209 West Houston Street, New York, NY 10014, www.filmforum.org).

# 2 __ 9/11 Tribute Museum

*Stories of survival and recovery*

In the years following the 9/11 terrorist attacks, onlookers flooded into lower Manhattan to see Ground Zero. But what they found were police barricades and other confused bystanders. They needed information. So in 2006, the 9/11 Families Association stepped in to fill the void. They established the 9/11 Tribute Museum to tell the story of that day through exhibits and walking tours led by volunteers, who share their first-hand experiences. "Most museums collect artifacts. We like to say we collect people," says Director of Programs, Kristine Pottinger.

The volunteers are family members, survivors, rescue and recovery workers, civilian volunteers, and local residents. Their stories help the rest of us understand. You begin your visit with rare videos of the day of the attack and recovery efforts afterwards. Carefully chosen objects highlight the human voice. The badly damaged firefighter's turnout gear belonged to Firefighter Jonathan Ielpi, son of Tribute co-founder Lee Ielpi. A smashed briefcase found in the rubble represents its owner Jim Geiger, who was evacuated from the North Tower's 51st floor. He remembers FBI agents saying, "Get as far away from the building and as fast as you can!"

The personal stories told live here make this museum truly unique. Volunteers sit on a stool in the story area and tell their truth. Listen to a son who lost his firefighter father in the attacks and worked on rebuilding the World Trade Center site. A survivor from the south tower honors the man who saved her at the cost of his own life. Or a woman whose husband died in the attack. In his honor, she now helps pay medical costs for children. These are the lives after 9/11.

Finally, we see a gallery showing all the companies, foundations, and non-profit organizations that have sprung up as a result of 9/11. They represent the ultimate spirit of service and resilience.

Retired Firefighter Lee Ielpi searches for his son Firefighter Jonathan Ielpi

"I met a lot of dads that were looking for their sons. Again, like we said, the fire service, it's a tradition that's passed down to your kids. There were a lot of sons that showed up to look for their dads. Nephews looking for uncles. About eight of us got together, dads, and stayed together. We were nicknamed the 'Band of Dads.' We would meet up in the morning, have a plan for the day. You realized that the devastation was so extensive."

**Lee Ielpi**
FIREFIGHTER, RESCUE 2 FDNY (RETIRED)
FATHER OF FDNY FIREFIGHTER JONATHAN IELPI

**Address** 92 Greenwich Street, New York, NY 10006, +1 (866)737-1184, www.911tributemuseum.org, info@911tributemuseum.org | **Getting there** Subway to Wall Street (4, 5), Rector Street (1, N, R, W) | **Hours** Mon–Sat 10am–6pm, Sun 10am–5pm | **Tip** Pay tribute to another survivor of the 9/11 attacks, a massive, 25-foot-tall, cast-bronze sculpture by German artist Fritz Koenig, called *The Sphere*. It was recovered from the rubble, damaged but mostly intact, and remains a symbol of strength (Liberty Park, 165 Liberty Street, New York, NY 10281).

# 3__Alice Austen House

*A picture perfect cottage*

If Alice Austen (1866–1952) were alive today, you can imagine that she would have a big social media following. Photography was her passion, and she was constantly taking pictures of family and friends in her upper-crust Staten Island milieu. Summer costume parties, groups of bustle-wearing women posing for the camera. Victorian life unplugged.

To visit her waterside cottage in Staten Island is to immerse yourself in the life of one of America's earliest and most prolific female photographers, who captured 8,000 images. Floor-to-ceiling windows open out over New York Harbor, with lovely boats passing by. Named "Clear Comfort," the house is where Alice lived with her life partner Gertrude Tate. Standing in the 1690 cottage today, with its low ceilings and patterned wallpaper, you feel the presence of her life and artistry. And also her independent spirit. Alice was a rebel, packing her heavy camera equipment onto her bicycle to pedal to the ferry. She took street photos of immigrants on the Lower East Side. A girl selling newspapers, an organ grinder and his wife, she took candid portraits showing humanity amidst the struggle. She was a photojournalist 40 years before the term was even coined.

Step out onto the sun porch, and you can leaf though albums of her work. It feels as if you are discovering a lost cache of images. In fact, it's lucky her glass negatives survived at all. While Alice enjoyed an affluent life, she lost everything in the 1929 stock market crash. She was so destitute that she was declared a pauper. Forced to sell this idyllic cottage and all her possessions in 1945, she called the Staten Island Historical Society to take her negatives. And there they sat until a researcher discovered them in 1950. They were published in a book, and in *Life Magazine*. Just before Alice died, she attended an exhibition of her work. It was sweet recognition indeed.

Address 2 Hylan Boulevard, Staten Island, NY 10305, +1 (718)816-4506, www.aliceausten.org | Getting there Staten Island Ferry, then S 51 bus (Bus Ramp B) to Hylan Boulevard and Bay Street | Hours Tue–Fri 1–5pm, Sat & Sun 11am–5pm | Tip Visit the little known Garibaldi-Meucci Museum to learn about an Italian refugee touted to be the true inventor of the telephone (420 Tompkins Avenue, Staten Island, NY 10305, www.garibaldimeuccimuseum.org).

# 4 American Folk Art Museum
*The art of everyday life*

It seems all of New York City has been rooting for the beloved American Folk Art Museum. It was right after 9/11 when they inaugurated a new home in Midtown. Financial difficulties followed, and they sold the building to the Museum of Modern Art. There was even talk of dispersing their unparalleled collection of folk and outsider art. But they scaled back and reopened in their current, smaller space near Lincoln Center. Finances improved, and now things seem better than ever.

With just three small galleries, it's easy to stop in regularly and take in the deftly curated exhibitions, which change during the year. The emphasis is on creative expression by self-taught artists, with fresh ideas, from both the past and the present. You will see objects here you won't see anywhere else, sometimes featuring pieces rarely on public view. You might see posthumous American portraiture, the very touching paintings of loved ones, created after a family member had died, like children posed with beloved pets in front of the family home, or sculptures of children who had perished. Even photo lockets of the departed. The idea was to create a lasting memory, a chance for the beloved to live on forever.

Other themes have focused on folk art and fashion, like a Folk Couture exhibition, where modern-day designers created contemporary fashions inspired by pieces from the museum's collection. Exhibits have delved into fairy tales via handmade books and sculpture. An exhibition with objects from Masonic societies delved into the cryptic signs, gestures, and arcane rituals of these fraternal clubs. All of the exhibitions are just slightly unusual.

Finally, don't miss the gift shop, with its own folk-inspired vibe. You'll find hooked rug pillows, stuffed animals made of recycled newspaper, glass intaglio cameo earrings, and folk art related books for children and adults.

Address 2 Lincoln Square, New York, NY 10023, +1 (212)595-9533,
www.folkartmuseum.org, info@folkartmuseum.org | Getting there Subway to 66th Street/
Lincoln Center (1); bus to Broadway/West 66th Street (M7), Broadway/West 63rd Street
(M20), West 65th Street/Columbus Avenue (M66) | Hours Tue–Thu 11:30am–7pm,
Fri noon–7:30pm, Sat 11:30am–7pm, Sun noon–6pm | Tip Walk across the street to see
the iconic Lincoln Center fountain, featured in movies like *Moonstruck* and *Ghostbusters*.
Recently renovated, the dazzling water columns go 40 feet high (10 Lincoln Center Plaza,
New York, NY 10023, www.lincolncenter.org).

# 5 American Museum of Natural History

*Where butterflies are free*

The American Museum of Natural History, founded in 1869, boasts over 34 million specimens and artifacts. One of the loveliest experiences here is the Butterfly Conservatory, a vivarium filled with hundreds of the colorful insects, flying around freely. And you get to join them. Open seasonally during the cooler months, the 1,200-square-foot enclosure admits small groups of visitors at a time. You enter through the double doors, pause, and then step inside through a second set of doors to ensure the butterflies don't escape.

Inside is filled with delights. Visitors walk along winding paths through the greenery, while all kinds of brightly colored butterflies flit and flutter about. It is startling and mesmerizing at the same time. The butterflies come from farms in Florida, Costa Rica, Kenya, and Thailand. Look for the iridescent blue morpho, which seem to change from blue to green before your eyes. The scarlet swallowtails pop with their black and red drama. And you can't take your eyes off the large owl butterflies with their mysterious eye-spotted wings.

The average life span for butterflies is just two to three weeks, so pupae are continually being shipped here from all over the world. A special glass case shows rows of pupae in various colors and stages. Watch as adult butterflies magically emerge from their chrysalises, to be released into the vivarium just hours later. The scene is spellbinding.

Docents attract butterflies to their hands and give fascinating facts about these beguiling creatures. As you leave to visit the rest of the museum, you pass through an enclosed vestibule with a floor-to-ceiling mirror. You are reminded to check your reflection to make sure you have no hitchhikers. "Take a good look," she sings. " They are tenacious little creatures."

**Address** Central Park West at 79th Street, New York, NY 10024, +1 (212)769-5100, www.amnh.org, info@amnh.org | **Getting there** Subway to 81st Street (B weekdays only, C), Broadway/West 79th Street (1) | **Hours** Daily Oct–May 10am–5:45pm; check website for exact dates | **Tip** Visit the storybook Belvedere Castle in Central Park, which offers stunning views of the city (middle of Central Park at 79th Street, New York, NY 10021).

# 6 Americas Society

*Art in a surreptitious mansion*

Designed in 1909 by McKim, Mead & White, the very building that hosts the Americas Society is a posh Park Avenue town home with Juliet balconies and classical columns – Upper East Side architecture at its best. Along with the two neighboring buildings, this area is one of the few remaining intact architectural pockets on Park Avenue.

That very architectural splendor is what attracts people to step inside. You will find a small viewing space just off the elegant lobby. Even though many New Yorkers don't even know it's here, this is the longest standing private gallery space in the US, dedicated to showing art from Latin America, the Caribbean, and Canada.

New exhibitions open three times per year, led by a host of guest curators from all over the world. That's what keeps it interesting. The idea is to show work that might not otherwise be seen in the United States, exploring artists and subjects that are not yet universally well known. You might find shows dedicated to Peruvian pottery, with masterpieces of pre-Colombian art. There have been exhibitions on cutting-edge, 21st-century portraiture. And exhibits have focused on the decorative arts as well, with mid-century modern furniture from Brazil, Mexico, and Venezuela. You will always see something compelling. Often you'll have the gallery to yourself, where you'll find a docent on hand to answer any questions. It feels like your own, private museum.

Attend one of their many concerts in the opulent, second-floor salon as well, where you feel the history of the home, first owned by financier Percy Rivington Pyne. But from 1947 to 1965, the grand estate served as a Soviet Mission to the United States, where Soviet Premier Nikita Khrushchev stayed for a period of time. And legend has it, when the Americas Society took over the building in 1966, electronic listening devices were found hidden in the walls.

Address 680 Park Avenue, New York, NY 10021, +1 (212)249-8950, www.as-coa.org |
**Getting there** Subway to 68th Street/Hunter College (6), Lexington Avenue/
63rd Street (F, Q) | **Hours** Wed–Sat noon–6pm | **Tip** Stop by Hauser & Wirth, a
Swiss art gallery, showing world-class contemporary artists, inside a chic, minimal
space (32 East 69th Street, New York, NY 10021, www.hauserwirth.com).

# 7 Asia Society

*Where the exotic and cutting edge collide*

Situated along Park Avenue is a surprising touch of the Far East on Manhattan's Upper East Side. Step into the Asia Society, and you've entered a far-away land, no plane ticket required. The galleries here immerse you in the ancient and the avant-garde. There is much to discover.

Founded in 1956 by John D. Rockefeller III, the idea was to promote better understanding of Asia through its art and culture. Rockefeller was a passionate collector of Asian art, and his acquisitions form the core of the Asia Society Museum Collection, which is admired across the world. Key pieces on view rotate but often include porcelain, ceramics, and metal works.

A highlight of this museum is the 15th-century Ming-period porcelain flask with vivid, cobalt-blue underglaze. Its lively, three-clawed dragon sweeps across the curved surface, a striking symbol of imperial power. It has a fragility about it but also a strength as an acclaimed masterpiece right before your eyes. So too with the handsome 16th-century square serving dish used in the Japanese art of serving tea. The milky, cream-colored glaze looks somehow modern, despite its great age. It is a visual play on the past and present.

Then juxtaposed with these ancient artifacts are the contemporary, rotating exhibitions featuring artists working today who are breaking boundaries of yesterday. It might be a group of drawings inspired by the Vietnam War, or a sculpture installation on political prisoners in Myanmar. The mixture underscores the deep history of Asia and its complex challenges.

For a special treat, have lunch in the peacefully appointed Asia Society Garden Court Café. With its glass roof and towering potted trees, it's like dining in a secret forest. Here you can escape the world while savoring the fine pleasures of sipping tea. Park Avenue throbs outside while you are happily ensconced in this lovely place.

Address 725 Park Avenue, New York, NY 10021, +1 (212)288-6400, www.asiasociety.org, info@asiasociety.org | Getting there Subway to East 68th Street/Hunter College (6), East 63rd Street/Lexington Avenue (F), 72nd Street (N, Q) | Hours Tue–Sun 11am–6pm year round, Fri 11am–9pm (Sept–June) | Tip Imagine you are in France with a visit to St. Jean Baptiste Catholic Church, where the glorious stained-glass windows were made in Chartres, France (184 East 76th Street, New York, NY 10021, www.stjeanbaptisteny.org).

# 8_ Bard Graduate Center

*Where objects tell a story*

Tucked inside a glorious townhouse, just steps from Central Park, the Bard Graduate Center Gallery is one of those addresses you're tempted to keep to yourself, a quiet, in-the-know kind of place, shared only with close friends. Understood. Push open the massive, iron front door with its graceful curves. Once you step through, you know you are someplace special. Inside, small galleries are located on the multiple floors of this six-story townhouse, accessed by vintage elevator or a stunning curved staircase. Simply maneuvering through the space is a joy. You may well have the galleries to yourself, allowing for quiet intimacy and great discovery.

Many museums focus on the fine arts of painting and sculpture. But here, objects are the key: how they are made, used, and displayed. You will see the intrinsically beautiful pieces, but also the everyday objects that tell so much about the way we live. Design history and material culture round out the focus.

Bard is a graduate center after all, so exhibitions are expertly re-searched and lavishly displayed, with thoughtfully designed galleries that inspire. Themes rotate, offering up the unexpected. Even exhi-bitions about things you may not know anything about pull you in with their insight and beauty. There is a special commitment to seek out little recognized topics and bring them to light. And because they often display objects borrowed from private collections, you may view treasures here that have never been seen in public at all.

Examples of past exhibitions include mid-century furniture by Finnish designers Alvar Aalto and Aino Marsio-Aalto, and the famed New York Crystal Palace of 1853. They've also explored hats, Swedish wooden toys, American Christmas cards, cloisonné, and Knoll textiles. It's this varied and thoughtful approach to objects that makes this museum a fresh voice in the aesthetic world, and a little address worth sharing.

Address 18 West 86th Street, New York, NY 10024, +1 (212)501-3019, www.bgc.bard.edu, gallery@bgc.bard.edu | Getting there Subway to 86th Street/Central Park West (B, C), 86th Street/Broadway (1) | Hours Tue, Fri–Sun 11am–5pm, Wed & Thu 11am–8pm (check website for exhibition times) | Tip With its soaring towers, the nearby Beresford is one of Manhattan's most celebrated, pre-war apartment buildings. Celebrities like Jerry Seinfeld, Beverly Sills, and Tony Randall have all lived here (211 Central Park West, New York, NY 10024).

# 9 BLDG 92

*An old shipyard made new again*

Set inside an industrial neighborhood near Williamsburg, BLDG 92 tells the fascinating story of the massive Brooklyn Navy Yard. Pass through the front gate of what used to be the Marine Commandant's residence. It's a modern museum, built in a modern way. The enormous, metal curtain on the building's façade is a high-tech sunscreen. It keeps the inside cool, and it also displays an image of a giant ship. This is form and function, Brooklyn style.

There's much to discover in this industrial space. Begin in the lobby, where an immense anchor weighing 22,500 pounds welcomes you aboard. The ultimate piece of found art, its huge chain reaches three stories up. Inside, we learn about this strip along the East River, known as Wallabout Basin. The British kept their prison ships here during the American Revolutionary War, positioned just off shore. Many American patriots died on those ships, their bodies tossed into the bay.

From 1801 to 1966, the Navy Yard functioned as an important shipbuilding center. Interactive exhibits focus on World War II, when this space was dubbed, the 'Can-Do Yard' because of the 70,000 people who worked here around the clock, building and adapting ships for war. You can hear testimonials from some of those men and women, who share their personal tales of long days and hard work. You'll also see some very big model ships that are detailed mock-ups of the vessels that were made right here.

You will also learn about the Navy Yard's business model today as an incubator where entrepreneurial spirit is alive. From bread bakers to winemakers and fashion to furniture, dozens of businesses manufacture their products in the Navy Yard. Be sure to stop by the ground-floor coffee shop, which features rotating exhibitions of some of the inventive products made here, including chairs, mirrors, sculptures, and tables.

Address 63 Flushing Avenue, Brooklyn, NY 11205, +1 (718)907-5932, www.brooklynnavyyard.org/visit/bldg-92, info@bnydc.org | Getting there Subway to York Street (F), Dekalb Avenue (B, N, Q, R) | Hours Wed–Sun noon–6pm | Tip Sample handmade bourbons and whiskeys in the secret tasting room of Kings County Distillery, the oldest in New York City, which now distills spirits in the Navy Yard gatehouses (229 Sands Street, Brooklyn, NY 11205, www.kingscountydistillery.com).

# 10   Bowne & Co. Stationers

*A printer with panache*

There was a time when a hand-printed piece of stationery was something special. Thick, luxurious paper displayed letters and designs pressed into the rich surface. You can experience that old-school art form once more in Lower Manhattan at this ever-charming print shop, a walk back in time. "We get excited here talking about typeface," confesses printer Christine Picone.

As you enter the atmospheric shop, one on one, printers are working right before your eyes. You'll watch as a giant, double-handled roller is pushed across a stone, covered with pitch-black ink. Then the 19th-century letterpress is put into play, and visitors can help turn the handle. Voilà, the finished print is there for you to feel, a tangible link to the 1800s right in your hands.

Bowne & Co. is New York's oldest business, operating under the same name since 1775. That's when this cobblestone street along the waterfront, was filled with small-batch printers meeting local merchants' endless need for paper and printed products. Today, it is run by the South Street Seaport Museum nearby. You feel the history here with the worn wooden countertops, stacks and stacks of printers drawers, and displays of luxurious stationery ready to touch. Then all around, there are various vintage presses to see, from Linotype to miniature tabletop versions.

Afterwards, head next door where they've recreated a vintage stationery store. Higgledy-piggledy, blank books, ledgers, writing papers, pens, inks, and pencils are piled high all around. Many of the cards here are printed in small batches right next door. Vintage brick walls display old photos of this very street through the ages. You have lost track of modern Manhattan completely.

Don't forget to say hello to printer Robert Warner in the back, who has been working here for more than 20 years. He's turned printing into a passion.

Address 211 Water Street, New York, NY 10038, +1 (646)315-4478, www.southstreetseaportmuseum.org | Getting there Subway to Fulton Street (A, C, J, Z, 2, 3, 4, 5) | Hours Daily 11am–7pm | Tip Check out the 60-foot-tall lighthouse at the Titanic Memorial. It was the brainchild of the famous 'unsinkable' survivor Molly Brown to commemorate the lives lost in the 1912 shipwreck (Fulton and Pearl Streets).

# 11___ *The Broken Kilometer*
*A polished stillness*

You have probably walked past this West Broadway doorway and had no idea what was hidden inside. But once you discover it, you won't likely forget it. Make your way into this street-level gallery and have a seat on one of the benches. You have just entered the SoHo art world of the late 1970s. It's been waiting for you all this time.

Within the white-walled space, with its Corinthian columns, is an art installation that covers the entire floor. Called *The Broken Kilometer*, it's composed of 500 highly polished brass rods in military alignment. The rods are arranged in five parallel rows of 100 rods each. But the trick lies in the spaces between the rods. As you move from front to back, that spacing increases by five millimeters. The result is a play on perspective. Instead of converging at a vanishing point, the rods appear perfectly parallel. It's the ultimate fusion of an artwork and the building itself, a glistening trompe l'oeil that is both mathematical and sublime.

The work has been inside this same gallery since 1979, when conceptual artist Walter De Maria (1935–2013), who also created the New York Earth Room (see ch. 79), placed it here in true minimalist style. This was a time when the SoHo gallery scene was thriving, before it was replaced by retail shopping in the 1990s. To witness the work inside this raw 1970s gallery space is to get a real sense of that exciting time.

The work was commissioned and has been maintained all these years by the Dia Art Foundation (see ch. 26 & 79), a low profile but powerful organization. They choose artists to support and stick with them. The idea is to present a work in a single space and let it stand the test of time. And while SoHo has changed drastically over the years, this quiet gallery has remained the same. It is a hidden secret, offering a fresh perspective on the complexities of art and the meditative stillness within.

# Dia Art Foundation
# Walter De Maria
# The Broken Kilometer, 1979

393 West Broadway
open Wednesday–Sunday
12–3 pm and 3:30–6 pm
closed summer months
www.diaart.org

Address 393 West Broadway, New York, NY 10012, www.diaart.org | Getting there
Subway to Prince Street (N, R, W), Broadway-Lafayette (B, D, F, M), Spring Street
(C, E), Houston Street (1) | Hours Sept–June Wed–Sun noon–6pm (closed 3–3:30pm),
see website for seasonal hours | Tip See iconic rock-and-roll photography from Blondie
to Prince at the Morrison Hotel Gallery (116 Prince Street, New York, NY 10012,
www.morrisonhotelgallery.com).

# 12 Bronx Museum of the Arts
*An urban experience*

Think of this innovative museum right on the Grand Concourse as an offshoot of the neighborhoods all around it. The museum collects and often shows contemporary artwork that reflects the diverse people who live here, many from Africa, Asia, and Latin America. The idea is to act as a gathering place for artists and residents, which is why the museum is free for all ages, making art accessible to everyone.

The Bronx has been the birthplace for a number of important artistic movements such as hip-hop, graffiti art, and Latin Jazz. So these topics may serve as creative touchstones that shape many of the museum's diverse offerings. The exhibitions are always changing but might include the highly layered, colorful, collage-like works of Puerto Rican born artist Angel Otero. Calling them "Elegies," the artist uses an oilskin technique in his abstract works on fabric to form a vivid textural display that combines painting and assemblage.

The works of Chinese American Martin Wong (1946–1999) have been featured here in a retrospective exhibition. The artist's meticulously rendered paintings chronicled New York's East Village art scene in the 1980s and included diaristic renderings of the Lower East Side's Latino community, Chinatown, and graffiti artists. Also on view here was a sculptural installation by artist Sarah Sze that was first featured in the US Pavilion for the 2013 Venice Biennale. Called *Triple Point*, the massive work used elements of painting, architecture, and installation to create an immersive environment.

You'll also find on tap here a roster of performances and events that are meant to spark a dialog around the subject or the performance itself. A night of spoken-word storytelling might focus on immigration and the American Dream. Their Project X featured a Bronx-based slam poetry team. Fierce Friday gatherings have featured dance performances, followed by a 'drink-n-draw' session.

Address 1040 Grand Concourse, Bronx, NY 10456, +1 (718)681-6000, www.bronxmuseum.org, info@bronxmuseum.org | Getting there Subway to 167th Street (B, D), 161st Street/Yankee Stadium (4) | Hours Wed–Sun 11am–6pm | Tip Sample Mexican food from Oaxaca at La Morada, a restaurant known for their savory mole sauces (308 Willis Avenue, Bronx, NY 10454, www.lamoradanyc.com).

# 13__Brooklyn Art Library

*A sketchbook world of wonder*

At the apex of Williamsburg cool is a library, art gallery, and museum all rolled into one. Floor-to-ceiling shelves host thousands of sketchbooks filled with the musings and private stories of people from all over the world. The idea is simple: send participants the same kind of blank sketchbook. They fill theirs out and send them back to Brooklyn, where they remain in this permanent, handmade, and deeply personal repository.

Started in 2006, there are more than 40,000 sketchbooks from participants young and old. Enter this simple storefront, and you're dwarfed by the sheer volume of texts, all identical, yet no two the same. In the center, vintage wooden tables and chairs beckon you to sit down and encourage you to take all the time you want.

Where to begin? Staff will pull sketchbooks for you to view based on theme, place, or material, along with one random book to keep the electricity of discovery alive. Pages are filled with graphite, conté, acrylic, marker, chalk, pastel, and watercolor. There are statements of love, political diatribes, and personal secrets, and pages folded into origami. Some are colorfully lyrical, others as detailed as an ancient text. They come from São Paulo to Singapore, Boston to Berlin. All are fascinating.

Started as a college endeavor that took off, the project's co-founder Steven Peterman says a shared intimacy is at the core of the library. "It's private, but public. And the works aren't on the wall, but held in your hand," he says.

There's also a mobile library, a custom bookmobile that brings sketchbooks all across the country, creating pop-up libraries in towns big and small. But there's nothing quite like a visit to the beguiling Brooklyn location, where the outside world disappears, and each turn of the page offers a fresh sense of discovery, connecting you with this global community.

Address 28 Frost Street, Brooklyn, NY 11211, +1 (718)388-7941, www.sketchbookproject.com, hello@sketchbookproject.com | Getting there Subway to Lorimer Street (L), Metropolitan Avenue (G) | Hours Wed–Sun 10am–6pm | Tip A short walk away, dive into the world of bean-to-bar chocolate at Mast Brothers Chocolate Shop, chocolatiers with a cult-like following (111 North 3rd Street, Brooklyn, NY 11249, www.mastbrothers.com).

# 14 Brooklyn Historical Society

*Where history is hip*

Brooklyn Heights is one of those perfect neighborhoods that locals like to keep secret, with its quiet streets, rows of charming brownstones, flower-filled window boxes, and cinematic views of the Manhattan skyline. Right in the midst of this village-like setting is the magnificent Brooklyn Historical Society. Its 1881 terracotta clad, Queen Anne-style building is adorned with busts of Christopher Columbus, William Shakespeare, and Michelangelo Buonarroti.

One step through the front door, and you can sense the history. Mosaic floors, carved pillars, bronze hardware – it feels like you are walking onto a movie set. And while the architecture reflects the old, the exhibitions craft the new. You might find a collection of rare, 1958 photos of former Brooklyn Heights resident Truman Capote, who lived nearby at 70 Willow Street, where he wrote *Breakfast at Tiffany's* and *In Cold Blood*. Other exhibits have included poignant letters home from Brooklynites who left in the 1860s to fight in the American Civil War – deeply personal messages to parents, sweethearts, and children.

You might learn about the secrets of the Brooklyn sewer system; the life of baseball player Jackie Robinson; or a fun look at family portraiture. Galleries are located across several floors, and each space has its own unique charm.

Be sure to end your visit in the ravishing Othmer Library, a sea of civility and polished woodwork among the rows and rows of sumptuous stacks. Like a mini Oxford or Cambridge on Pierrepont Street, the double-height reading room is rimmed with stained-glass lunettes that flood colored light beams into the space. Brass lamps and chandeliers are topped with frosted-glass orbs. Additionally, the historical society hosts a fascinating range of public events – and even weddings.

**Address** 128 Pierrepont Street, Brooklyn, NY 11201, +1 (718)222-4111, www.brooklynhistory.org | **Getting there** Subway to Borough Hall (2, 3, 4, 5), Jay Street/Borough Hall (A, C, F), Court Street (R) | **Hours** Wed–Sun noon–5pm | **Tip** Take a stroll along the iconic Promenade, which offers heart-stopping views of the Manhattan skyline and the Brooklyn Bridge. You may recognize the views from classic movies *Annie Hall* and *Moonstruck*, among others (enter at Montague Street & Pierrepont Place, Brooklyn, NY 11201, www.nycgovparks.org).

# 15 Brooklyn Museum

*Wandering behind the scenes*

With its temple-like entrance framed by lush Prospect Park, the Brooklyn Museum may be considered the borough's cultural epicenter. The 1895 Beaux Arts building by McKim, Mead & White is classicism at its finest. And with a collection of more than 1.5 million pieces, only a small fraction of the works is on view.

What about all the rest? That's where a little-known corner on the fifth floor shines. Visiting the Visible Storage-Study Center, housed in the Luce Center for American Art, is a bit like being a museum worker rummaging around in the back room. Part storage facility, part public gallery, the space is densely packed with paintings, sculptures, furniture, ceramics, lamps, tiles, and pewter. With thousands of objects on view, it is a giant cabinet of curiosities, with one exciting discovery after another.

Glassed bays contain paintings mounted on rolling racks. Landscape paintings massed together on a wall allow you to see side-by-side comparisons of color, composition, and brushstroke. Dozens of sculptures lined up in glass vitrines dazzle with the sheer variety. Dense assortments of sterling silver positively sparkle. And because this is a working facility, all pieces are maintained at the proper conditions of humidity, temperature, and levels of light. Visible storage offers an inside look at how museums work.

Make sure you go see the Small Wonders section, where diminutive objects are displayed in a series of drawers. Pull one out, and then another, to see medals, jewelry, embroidery, and even flatware. It's like rifling through the Queen's attic. And don't miss the fetching red and white Spacelander Bicycle, a fiberglass and metal marvel. Manufactured in 1960, the unique design stores downhill energy, releasing it on uphill climbs. The bike is just one of the hidden delights in this back room treasure chest, where you get to be curator for the day.

Address 200 Eastern Parkway, Brooklyn, NY 11238, +1 (718)638-5000, www.brooklynmuseum.org, information@brooklynmuseum.org | Getting there Subway to Eastern Parkway/Brooklyn Museum (2, 3) | Hours Wed, Fri–Sun 11am–6pm, Thu 11am–10pm | Tip With more than 500 majestic acres, the lovely walking trails in the beloved Prospect Park are yours to discover (directly behind the museum, www.prospectpark.org).

# 16_ The Burns Archive

*Diving into the darker side*

The Burns Archive is one of those quirky outings you're not sure about at first, but then you tell all your friends about it afterwards. It's a Murray Hill brownstone owned by a practicing ophthalmologist. He's collected more than a million old photos, documenting the hidden side of death, medicine, and war. Unseen, forgotten, and disquieting images provide a powerful truth. "I'm a historian, not a collector," Dr. Stanley B. Burns says, "and photos provide irrefutable evidence."

Ring the buzzer at the vine-covered red door, and enter the ground-floor waiting room. Here the immersion begins. Framed images fill every inch of wall space, floor to ceiling, top to bottom. Medical maladies, early operating rooms, war battlefields – should you look, or turn away? Dr. Burns and his daughter and collaborator Elizabeth A. Burns greet you for the private tour and give an overview. They are a lively pair, ready with facts and stories, and sometimes finishing each other's sentences. They are the passionate caretakers of this curious collection.

Follow them to the second floor, and you've entered the heart of the archive. It's an overflowing, artifact-laden, working office, where vintage desks are heaped with folders, cards, post-it notes, books, magazines, and boxes.

The saffron-colored walls hold hundreds of photos: bereavement images, an X-ray of a serial killer's brain, medical dissections. Closets are stacked with archival boxes; drawers are filled with daguerreotypes. It's an overwhelming, at times disturbing, visual world, and you are brought right into the center of it. This encyclopedic knowledge is why Dr. Burns consults for movies and historical dramas. He's written countless books as well. And one-on-one, he brings visitors here to show them his life's work. As the good doctor likes to remind us, "Human nature has not changed."

Address 140 East 38th Street, New York, NY 10016, +1 (212)889-1938, www.burnsarchive.com | Getting there Subway to Grand Central/42nd Street (4, 5, 6, 7) | Hours Call to arrange a private tour | Tip Catch episodes of the HBO/Cinemax historical hospital drama, *The Knick*, or PBS's *Mercy Street*, as Dr. Burns was a consultant.

# 17 _ C.V. Starr Bonsai Museum

*A tiny museum for tiny trees*

The lusciously landscaped Brooklyn Botanic Garden is one of New York City's most beloved destinations, with its allées of blooming cherry trees, paths of roses and rhododendrons. Tucked in a corner inside a glass conservatory are the oldest trees in the garden, which also happen to be the smallest ones.

Enter, and the scent of moist earth envelopes you. Propped on wooden tables all around are miniature but absolutely mature trees twisted with mottled bark. With nearly 400 specimens, this is one of the largest bonsai collections on public display outside Japan. The tiny trees thrive inside this light-filled space, and each one is a wonder to see.

Great patience is what it takes to watch over these living works of art. Precise pruning encourages a thick root system, and in time, the bonsai believes it is a 30-foot-tall timber in a life-sized landscape. "Each tree has its own horticultural and seasonal needs," curator David Castro says, "they must be treated on a tree by tree basis." That means careful attention to watering, pruning or pinching, and fertilizing. Trees are kept in shallow pots to provide better airflow to the roots. Every few years the tiny trees are taken out of their pots for a root trim and then replanted with fresh soil.

Trees are trained to grow upright, slanted or in a grove. One Japanese white pine is 300 years old and is often displayed during the winter. A Trident Maple with pointed leaves, a gift to New York City from the City of Tokyo, is 140 years old. And the tiniest lilac tree actually has pink blossoms in the spring from its gracefully arching branches. "Spring, summer, fall, and winter each have their magical exhibition of colors, scents, foliage, and even lack of foliage to show off," Castro reminds us. Bonsai represents a delicate balance of energy meant to capture a quiet moment in nature in the smallest of forms.

Address 990 Washington Avenue, Brooklyn, NY 11225, +1 (718)623-7200, www.bbg.org | Getting there Subway to Eastern Parkway/Brooklyn Museum (2, 3), Prospect Park (B, Q, S), Franklin Avenue (4, 5) | Hours Tue–Fri 8am–6pm, Sat & Sun 10am–6pm | Tip A rose is way more than a rose in the nearby Cranford Rose Garden. It has more than 1,000 varieties, and is one of the largest rose collections in North America. Designed in 1927, the garden suffered devastating losses from rose rosette disease in 2009. Visit today to see the extensive restorations since then.

# 18_ Center for Book Arts
*Bound for glory*

It is always a joy to discover a very hidden place in New York City, and this is one of them. There amidst the tee shirt and trim shops in the Flatiron neighborhood, on the third floor of a nondescript office building, is the Center for Book Arts. When the elevator doors open, you've stepped right into a hidden atelier, a working studio and exhibition space where the making of books is an art form. "We want to attract people with the exciting work on display," founder Richard Minsky explains. "Then we show people they can make books too."

A small glassed-in gallery features an intriguing array of books, many made right here. These are not books about art. Here, the books are the art. Collated scraps of paper, bound like secret diaries. Renderings on translucent sheets, layered together. Long, foldout accordion pages. Even an American hymnal, with the musical notes delicately cut out like lace. The idea here is to stretch the boundaries of what a book can be. You begin asking yourself, "How is this a book? And is that one too?"

Perhaps best of all, you are actually encouraged to touch some of the works on view here. Little white gloves are provided for you to put on, allowing you to feel the lavish papers and beautiful bindings. "The tactile element is all part of it," Minsky says. "It's hard to understand a book without turning its pages."

Exit the gallery into the studio, and you are standing right in the middle of a beehive of activity. Master printers, artists, and students are hard at work in this dreamy, light-filled studio. Worn wooden floors, long working tables piled high. Vintage letterpresses line the room, and printers drawers are stacked everywhere. This is not an over-polished, gentrified space, but a real working studio operating since 1974. Enjoy a rare glimpse into an evolving art form that is anything but 'by the book.'

**Address** 28 West 27th Street, New York, NY 10001, +1 (212)481-0295, www.centerforbookarts.org | **Getting there** Subway to 28th Street/Broadway (N, R, W), 23rd Street/6th Avenue (F), 28th Street/Lexington Avenue (6), 28th Street/7th Avenue (1) | **Hours** Mon–Fri 11am–6pm, Sat 10am–5pm | **Tip** M&J Trimmings features a dizzying collection of buttons, bows, rhinestones, and lace. It's a vivid display that feels like a mini museum of DIY fashion and design (1008 6th Avenue, New York, NY 10018, www.mjtrim.com).

# 19_ Center for Italian Modern Art

*See art like a collector*

The elevator of this discrete SoHo building not only transports you to the fourth floor but also to a chic, private apartment in Milan. That's the idea behind the Center for Italian Modern Art, where you see art from a collector's point of view. Upon arrival, guests are invited into the kitchen, with its sleek, black Italian cabinetry and a Gio Ponti table. You are offered a cup of espresso to get the creative juices flowing. "We do things a little differently here," says director Heather Ewing. "Our ethos is to be more like a home."

The center is the brainchild of Italian art collector and scholar Laura Mattioli, who grew up surrounded by Italian masterpieces. Her father Gianni Mattioli purchased an apartment in Milan just to house his growing art collection. Then on Sundays, he opened it to the public and acted as tour guide himself. That's the inspiration for this unusual art space that is part museum, part home.

The Center features one exhibition for the year, with most pieces pulled from the family's collection. The works are hung throughout the airy, loft-like space, which is decorated with streamlined, Italian furniture. It's the dream apartment you wish you owned, and a perfect place to see art in an intimate setting.

Education is important here, with several international fellows doing research. The scholars give small private tours, and their enthusiasm is infectious. "Graduates have a different kind of experience, living with the works throughout the day," Ewing explains, "much like a collector." 20th-century artists like Giorgio de Chirico, or Giorgio Morandi have been on view in exhibits with many works that have never been seen in the US. The idea is to increase awareness of these modern Italian artists by connecting with them on a personal level. After the espresso, the apartment, and the art, you'll wish you could stay for dinner.

Address 421 Broome Street, 4th floor, New York, NY 10013, +1 (646)370-3596, www.italianmodernart.org, info@italianmodernart.org | Getting there Subway to Spring Street (6), Prince Street (R, W), Broadway/Lafayette Street (B, D, F, M), Canal Street (6, J, N, Q, R, W) | Hours Fri & Sat 11am–noon & 1–6pm, see website for tour times | Tip If all that Italian art made you hungry, head to Peasant, an intimate, rustic Italian restaurant with wood-fired dishes (194 Elizabeth Street, New York, NY 10012, www.peasantnyc.com).

# 20 Chaim Gross Studio
*Art and life, curated*

Ring the bell, and step into this hidden artist's studio and home in Greenwich Village. This is where renowned sculptor Chaim Gross (1904–1991) lived and worked for 28 years, and you are his guest. His home was also a gathering place for artists and intellectuals from the 1960s and 70s. Welcome to the club.

The studio looks like something out of a French film, with its Parisian-style skylight filling the space. It's as if the sculptor had just stepped away. Known for his expressionistic pieces, often in wood, Gross's workbench is here, along with dozens of beloved tools, all hanging in a row. Lyrical drawings line the wall, and a woodpile sits in the corner. This is where the Austrian immigrant created his towering, figurative sculptures that are a marvel to see in the round.

Then take the elevator up to the private apartment on the third floor and enter a personal art gallery, filled with surprises. The sculptor moved here in 1963 with his beloved wife and muse Renee (1909–2005). Floor to ceiling, front to back, the living space is filled with paintings, sculptures, and objects, all collected and arranged by the artist himself, just as he left them. Works on the walls are by Willem de Kooning, Marsden Hartley, Louise Nevelson, Stuart Davis, and Arshile Gorky. Many of these artists were friends of Gross and represent a who's who of 20th-century art. MoMA would be envious (see ch. 67). It's easy to imagine lively dinners and gatherings in this eclectic space. A wall of photos show the couple's circle of friends. Here is Gross posing next to Marilyn Monroe. And with Andy Warhol. Then more admirers like Helena Rubinstein, Allen Ginsberg, Barbra Streisand, and even Helen Keller. It's a rare chance to be immersed in the history of the Greenwich Village art scene and to see the working life of a sculptor who carved out a most remarkable legacy.

Address 526 LaGuardia Place, New York, NY 10012, +1 (212)529-4906,
www.rcgrossfoundation.org, info@rcgrossfoundation.org | Getting there Subway to
Bleeker Street (6), Broadway-Lafayette Street (B, D, F, M), West 4th Street (A, C, E) |
Hours By guided tour only, see website for details | Tip Experience a classic New York
deli reimagined in a modern way, at Sadelle's, where they stack freshly baked bagels on
wooden sticks attached to the walls (463 West Broadway, New York, NY 10012,
www.sadelles.com).

# 21 Children's Museum of Manhattan

*Where play has a purpose*

You would be forgiven if you longed to go back to your childhood after visiting this fun- and play-filled museum. With five floors of engaging exhibitions, the emphasis is on the arts, sciences, and the humanities. "Learn by playing" is the credo here.

Get the party started in the Let's Dance! exhibit, where the art of movement kicks into high gear. Little ones can try on tutus and costumes and then interact with an immersive video projection dome, where they can actually watch and dance along with professionals. Dancers from Alvin Ailey American Dance Theater come to life on the screen, along with many others, including the Ballet Hispánico and The Mark Morris Dance Group. It's all step-by-step. Another experience is a chance to create multicolor shadow dances.

Imagination is key to the 4,000-square-foot PlayWorks space. Children who are about to start school will discover problem-solving activities that teach and entertain. Here they will learn language and their ABCs with Alphie, a bright green, talking dragon, who eats letters of the alphabet. Nearby, city life is mimicked with a fire truck and an MTA bus. A sand area explores sculpture and texture.

Clever exhibits are entertaining, and they also teach positive, lifelong habits. At EatSleepPlay, healthy eating and daily rituals are played out in purposeful ways. Little ones are inspired to fall in love with vegetables through a unique, interactive biology exhibit. Toddlers can actually crawl through a playground-like, giant digestive system, which follows nutrients through the body. They can also meet the charming Super Sprowtz, a team of super powered vegetable heroes that make eating fruits and vegetables fun. Then finally, everyone can get exercising together by pedaling and running to encourage a life of daily movement for kids of all ages.

**Address** 212 West 83rd Street, New York, NY 10024, +1 (212)721-1223, www.cmom.org, info@cmom.org | Getting there Subway to 79th or 86th Street (1), 81st or 86th Street (B, C) | Hours Tue–Fri & Sun 10am–5pm, Sat 10am–7pm | Tip Visit the spectacular Hayden Planetarium, a giant, 87-foot-diameter orb that appears to be floating in a glass cube. You can't take your eyes off it, and seeing from the inside is even better (Rose Center for Earth and Space, 175–208 79th Street, Central Park West, NY 10024, www.amnh.org).

# 22 The City Reliquary Museum

*Where thousands of objects find a permanent home*

If you like orderly, minimal spaces this is not the place for you. But if you fancy jam-packed, cover-every-inch places, you will feel right at home in this little Williamsburg storefront. It started in 2002 as a window display in Dave Herman's apartment. Now it's a permanent museum crammed full of artifacts, all about New York City.

Prepare yourself for a Statue of Liberty tsunami, hundreds and hundreds of them, made into the most curious objects. There are Lady Liberty plates, pendants, and paper weights. Thimbles, thermometers, frames, magnets, cake molds, and beer openers. Even a Statue of Liberty grotto in the back garden, with Lady Liberty in a bathtub, much like the lawn shrines of the Virgin Mary in a bathtub. "A reliquary usually contains a sacred or religious object," Herman says. "But the Statue of Liberty is our secular saint of the New York Harbor. She's a symbol of the city that's for everyone."

You'll also find displays on the World's Fair, Brooklyn seltzer bottles, and New York City bridges. But it's the burlesque display that tantalizes. It's inside a metal locker that is lined with red silk and lit with a mini crystal chandelier. This is where you'll find a shrine to early 20th-century exotic dancer Little Egypt, who inspired all those who came afterwards. We see photos of her posing with veils. Then press a button, and a dancing burlesque mannequin performs the Hootchie Kootchie, right on the spot, spangly brassiere and all.

Finally look for a small glass vessel labeled NYC Subway Rail Dust. It's filled with microscopic metal particles, the residue that results when subway wheels scrape the metal rails. "It's dangerous to inhale, and only subway workers and firefighters know about it," says Herman, who happens to be a former firefighter. "Its one of my favorite pieces here – one of those obscure by-products of daily, city life."

Address 370 Metropolitan Avenue, Brooklyn, NY 11211, +1 (718)782-4842,
www.cityreliquary.org | Getting there Subway to Metropolitan Avenue (G), Lorimer
Street (L), Marcy Avenue (J, M, Z) | Hours Thu–Sun noon–6pm | Tip Hang out with
the Williamsburg music cognoscenti at the legendary Knitting Factory, where you can
hear indie-rock, hip-hop, and cutting edge vocalists (361 Metropolitan Avenue,
Brooklyn, NY 11211, www.bk.knittingfactory.com).

# 23 Coney Island Museum

*A world of fun under the sun*

There is something about a trip to Coney Island that never disappoints. Bright colors, bold rides, broad beaches. But many people don't realize that there's a secret Coney Island museum along the iconic Surf Avenue. It's inside a 100-year-old building, and it's filled with nostalgic treasures from 'The People's Playground.'

In the early 1900s, throngs of new American immigrants were flooding to Coney Island in search of fun and sun. The museum at the top of the creaky, painted staircase transports you back to that era. We see some of the old ride cars here, like a charming, red and yellow, wooden Whip Car. You can imagine all the sweaty hands holding tight to its metal safety bar. Nearby, a handsome, 1925 wicker Rolling Chair is upholstered with green and white striped ticking fabric. These rickshaw-like rolling chairs were the queens of the boardwalk.

By the 1920s, the new Coney Island subway made this destination extremely popular, a paradise beach resort for New York's working class. People living in harsh tenements now had the chance to escape the searing city heat. They arrived by the thousands, sometimes the millions, on any given summer day. 'Sea bathing' was the thing to do here, and the museum features vintage wool swimsuits and trunks, which could be rented for the afternoon. Fetching black-and-white photos show groups of women and couples, posing proudly in their bathing attire. Nearby, dozens of vintage plaid thermoses and metal coolers show us early beach accoutrements.

Then see the rare hold-to-light postcards in gold shadow box frames along the wall. Sold in souvenir shops in the 1890s, they are a wonder even today. Push the little light switch on the wall, and you see the amusement park in bright sun. Flip the switch, and a light from behind shows the same scene, but at night with the carnival rides magically lit up, Wonder Wheel and all.

Address 1208 Surf Avenue, 2nd Floor, Brooklyn, NY 11224, +1 (718)372-5159, www.coneyisland.com | Getting there Subway to Stilwell Avenue (D, F, N, Q) | Hours Summer Wed–Sat noon–6pm, Sun 2–6pm; off-season Sat noon–6pm, Sun 2–6pm | Tip On the ground floor of the Coney Island USA building, have a drink at the groovy Freak Bar, offering Coney Island Brewing Company beers and hard sodas. You may even meet a mermaid, a snake charmer, or a strongman (1208 Surf Avenue, Brooklyn, NY 11224, www.coneyislandusa.com).

# 24_Cooper Hewitt
*Where you're the designer*

How do you turn a massive, Gilded Age mansion into a trendy design museum? You fill it with fun, interactive elements and let the visitor be the designer. That's the 21st-century mission of this Smithsonian museum, where product design is *de rigueur*. Upon entering, you are handed a tricked out electronic pen that will be your tool throughout your visit. At table-size touchscreens, click the pen on pieces from the collection to explore. Click another button, and you can draw your own version of the object right on the screen. It's completely addictive. Then once you are home, plug the number on your admission ticket into the museum website. You'll find that the images you saved on your pen are there waiting for you. Just like design magic.

Equally as engaging is the Immersion Room, where the museum's extensive collection of wall coverings actually materialize before your eyes. Choose a pattern on the touch screen. Instantly, it is electronically projected floor-to-ceiling and onto the walls all around. With the push of a button, the patterns change, offering an eye popping experience. This is wallpaper as theater.

While modernity is the mantra here, you never lose sight of the Old World. Galleries are set inside this impossibly grand, 1902 Andrew Carnegie-built estate. The industrial magnate had a penchant for exotic woods and ornate chandeliers, which contrast beautifully with the tech-driven displays – a visual yin and yang.

As you walk through the galleries, you'll be smitten with the many objects of desire on view. Pieces rotate from the collection and exhibits might include the mod 1967 red Tongue Chair; a 1930s chrome and enamel Smoker's Tray; or a delicate, silver choker. All of these pieces carry a design panache. Don't miss the glorious, glass period conservatory just off the gift shop. With splendid garden views, it is hidden New York at its best.

Address Cooper Hewitt, Smithsonian Design Museum, 2 East 91st Street, New York, NY 10128, +1 (212)849-8400, www.cooperhewitt.org | Getting there Subway to 86th Street/Lexington Avenue (4, 5, 6), 96th Street/Lexington Avenue (6) | Hours Mon–Fri & Sun 10am–9pm, Sat 10am–9pm | Tip Have a sinful lunch at the Bluestone Lane Café, an Australian-style coffee shop adjacent to the Episcopal Church Of Heavenly Rest (1085 5th Avenue, New York, NY 10128, www.bluestonelane.com).

# 25 Daredevil Tattoo Museum

*For the love of ink*

In the midst of Chinatown's hustle and bustle, you'll find a hidden temple to the humble tattoo. Daredevil Tattoo is a working tattoo shop and a museum all in one. "I love the community of tattooing and the history of it," says co-owner Michelle Myles.

Through the front door, floor-to-ceiling cases contain one of the world's most significant collections of tattoo history. It's a New York story that began in the Lower East Side neighborhood, just blocks from here. You'll see rare photos of so-called tattooed ladies, the working-class women who performed in sideshows and circuses. We see a 19th-century photo of Nora Hildebrandt, who showed off her inked body. She famously claimed that Native Americans took her captive and tattooed her by force. Nearby, Millie Hull strikes a sassy, 1930s pose with her red lips and head-to-toe tattoos. She later became a tattoo artist herself, working out of the back of a barber shop.

Also on hand is the precursor to today's tattoo machine. It's an 1876 Thomas Edison-motorized engraving pen that was originally meant for paper surfaces but was frequently used for tattooing too. All around, you'll see highly detailed tattoo designs, from minimal to magical. There are hundreds and hundreds of them. These delicately rendered images come from Europe, while those thickly outlined drawings show the bolder, American style of tattooing. Simple flowers, snakes, dragons, hearts, flags, action characters, and fancy script create a visual vocabulary meant for human skin.

Meanwhile, customers amble in and out of the shop, booking appointments and finalizing designs. Once a seedy neighborhood, it is now more mainstream, much like tattoos themselves. You are immersed in the world of the illustrated human body and the contemporary culture that has blossomed around it.

Address 141 Division Street, New York, NY 10002, +1 (212)533-8303, www.daredeviltattoo.com | Getting there Subway to East Broadway (F), Grand Street (B, D), Essex Street (J, M) | Hours Daily noon–10pm | Tip Indulge your sense of urban adventure with a walk across the Manhattan Bridge. It is a bit more industrial looking than the Brooklyn Bridge, but less crowded. The views are Instagram-worthy, and the graffiti art changes regularly (pedestrians enter at Forsyth & Canal Streets).

# 26__Dia:Chelsea
*A visionary voyage*

Many of New York's most compelling, long-term art installations exist because of one institution: The Dia Art Foundation, a behind-the-scenes but powerful organization that chooses artists to support and doggedly sticks with them. You feel that singular focus when entering the Dia exhibition spaces in Chelsea. Unlike the sleek art galleries all around, this former marble-cutting facility has been left raw, as if you are discovering something abandoned.

But once inside, you are viewing art that pushes boundaries. They have shown the shades-of-white canvases by Robert Ryman, or the sculptural installations by Kishio Suga that play off balance and structure. Exhibitions here are well curated and thought provoking.

Dia was founded in 1974 by Philippa de Menil, Heiner Friedrich, and Helen Winkler. The idea was to help artists create visionary projects that might not otherwise be realized because of scale or scope. Many of these artists emerged in the 1960s and 70s, and Dia collected them in depth, committing to show their work for the long-term. Today, Dia has many sites, from New York, to the American Southwest, to Germany. The jewel in the crown is Dia:Beacon, 60 miles north of New York City, where an abandoned Nabisco factory has been turned into a world-class museum, showing artists like Agnès Martin and Carl Andre. Without the backing of Dia, beloved permanent SoHo exhibitions like Walter De Maria's New York Earth Room (see ch. 79) would not be possible.

The Dia:Chelsea space uniquely serves as an incubator for ideas going forward. More women artists are being brought into the fold, along with artists on a global scale. And you're just as likely to find poetry readings here, along with concerts. So while the Chelsea galleries nearby are trying to sell art, Dia is staying true to its mission to support art and allowing the works to speak over time.

Address 535, 541, 545 West 22nd Street, New York, NY 10011, +1 (212)989-5566, www.diaart.org, info@diaart.org | Getting there Subway to 23rd Street (1, A, C, E) | Hours Tue–Sat 11am–6pm | Tip With its cool Latin vibe, the rooftop lounge of Hotel Americano is the perfect perch for a post gallery drink (518 West 27th Street, New York, NY 10001, www.hotel-americano.com).

# 27 — The Drawing Center
*Sketching it out*

Sometimes the humble drawing gets lost in the great big art world. Installations and massive oil paintings often steal the show. But drawing is where art began. And, as it turns out, it is shaping the future of art as well. That's where the Drawing Center comes in. This institution has taken the idea of drawing and turned it upside down with its exhibits and unique programs.

Housed in a classic SoHo building, a renovated 19th-century, cast-iron beauty, the Drawing Center feels modern and fresh. Inside the lobby you'll see the airy bookstore with floor-to-ceiling shelves. This is your amuse-bouche – a small tasting of catalogs showing the kinds of exhibitions they mount in this space. Stacked top to bottom, the volumes are beautifully bound with tantalizing covers. Peruse the possibilities.

Then make your way into the galleries straight ahead, where changing exhibitions surprise and inspire. For example, Thread Lines unraveled the idea of line by connecting it to textiles. With sewing, knitting, and weaving, artists created a variety of works that shifted the possibility of line into a new context. They have done the same with video, making the hand-drawn come to life. So-called animated drawings by Amy Sillman overlay renderings on paper with iPhone and iPad sketches. Artist Cecily Brown approached drawing as a way of seeing. With her Rehearsal exhibition, she drew the same images over and over again, as if rehearsing. She drew clip-art images repeatedly, which became a daily activity.

Meanwhile, the Center's Open Sessions get creative minds exploring what drawing will become. Select artists are chosen for two-year cycles, where they debate and collaborate, and even share their works in progress. Afterwards, the most forward thinking ideas are turned into exhibitions for everyone to see. So sharpen your pencils for that.

Address 35 Wooster Street, New York, NY 10013, +1 (212)219-2166, www.drawingcenter.org, info@drawingcenter.org | Getting there Subway to Canal Street (1, 6, A, C, E, J, N, Q, R, W) | Hours Wed, Fri–Sun noon–6pm, Thu noon–8pm | Tip Fantasize about completely reorganizing your entire home at the minimalist Japanese store Muji SoHo, where order is an art form (455 Broadway, New York, NY 10013, www.muji.com).

# 28 Ellis Island Immigration Museum

*Go inside the island of tears*

With its red-brick grandeur, the French Renaissance Revival building on Ellis Island must have been very intimidating to the nervous immigrants arriving in New York Harbor. More than 12 million people passed through this great hall between 1892 and 1954. It's easy to imagine how arduous their journey was. Ellis Island was the gateway to their new lives.

The beautifully curated Immigration Museum is managed by the National Park Service. There is much to see here, but it's the small objects that feel the most personal. Immigrants crowded into the baggage room upon their arrival. You will see a wall of luggage piled high with trunks made of wood, wicker, and metal. These people's entire lives may have been contained in a single chest.

The Treasures From Home exhibit reveals what was inside those trunks, the cherished belongings carried from the Old World to the new. We see bibles and prayer books, beloved crockery, and hand-sewn family linens. The most touching is a mohair and cotton teddy bear that belonged to a 10-year-old girl named Gertrude Schneider, who arrived in the United States in 1921. The bear was a gift from her uncle to console her after her favorite porcelain doll broke, and she donated it to the museum in 1988. We also see a family's feather bed and children's clothing.

Take a look at the recreated dormitory, where utilitarian, multi-tiered bunk beds have mattresses of canvas or mesh. Like stacked books on shelves, thousands of people slept here while waiting to enter the country. They had to answer questions and pass medical exams. And those with criminal, health, or psychological issues were turned away. They called it The Island of Tears, despite the hope that awaited them just across the harbor.

# Gertrud's Bear

Cuddly stuffed "Teddy" bears, like the one Gertrud Schneider received from her uncle after her favorite porcelain doll broke, developed simultaneously around the turn of the twentieth century in both Europe and America.

Morris and Rose Michtom of Brooklyn, New York, created a stuffed toy bear inspired by a popular cartoon of Theodore Roosevelt, then President of the United States, refusing to shoot a baby bear during a hunting trip. The couple received permission from Roosevelt to use his nickname, Teddy, for their stuffed bears.

About the same time, Richard Steiff, a German artist and animal lover who worked at his aunt's toy business, created a similar bear. The toy bear became extremely popular in both Europe and America.

Address Ellis Island National Museum of Immigration, New York, NY 10004, www.nps.gov/ellis | Getting there Departing from Battery Park, Statue Cruises takes you to Ellis Island | Hours Daily, Manhattan ferry departures 9:30am – 3:30pm | Tip Ferries also stop at Liberty Island, where you can see the Statue of Liberty up close. Be prepared – the sheer enormity and majesty of this iconic figure is unforgettable (www.libertyellisfoundation.org).

# 29__Explorers Club

*Lions and tigers and bears – oh my!*

People walking past this Upper East Side Jacobean-style townhouse have no idea about the wild things lurking inside. A giant stuffed polar bear named Percy. An Antarctic penguin. A cheetah from Teddy Roosevelt's 1909 African expedition. They are artifacts from great adventures across the globe set inside an impossibly grand, English-styled house. Who could resist?

"We're still a bit of a mystery to people," confesses Lacey Flint, archivist and curator of research collections. Founded in 1904, this private club is where the world's top explorers have gathered to trade tales. Past members Robert Peary and Mathew Henson were the first to reach the North Pole in 1909. Member Sir Edmund Hillary was the first person to summit Mt. Everest with Tenzing Norgay in 1953. Neil Armstrong and Buzz Aldrin, also members, reached the moon in 1969.

You feel that sense of discovery in the sumptuous surroundings, where artifacts of adventure are everywhere. In the red Members' Lounge, two enormous elephant tusks flank the fireplace. A massive, antique globe was actually used to plan historic expeditions. And those thick mittens are from the 1909 North Pole expedition. Wood-paneled walls and stained-glass windows add an air of aristocracy. Exoticism even extends to the club's legendary dinners, where tarantulas have been on the menu, along with other species like the iguana.

Any visit to the club culminates on the top floor, the ultimate hide-out with soaring ceilings, leather couches, handsome oil paintings. You are surrounded by taxidermy from all over the world; a walrus, a rhinoceros, a lion, and more. "All of these animals were collected for scientific study," Flint reminds us. Take everything in. And before you leave, find the Famous Firsts plaque in the lobby, listing pioneering expeditions. There's a blank space at the bottom for the first member to walk on Mars.

Address 46 East 70th Street, New York, NY 10021, +1 (212)628-8383, www.explorers.org |
Getting there Subway to Lexington Avenue/63rd Street (Q), Lexington Avenue/59th Street
(N, R), 68th Street (6) | Hours Call to book a private tour | Tip Rub shoulders with posh
art curators and scholars at the exquisitely appointed Frick Art Reference Library (10 East
71st Street, New York, NY 10021, www.frick.org).

# 30__Fraunces Tavern Museum

*A toast to independence*

With well-suited Wall Street financiers strutting by, this early American tavern appears out of time and place. And it is. But what happened here laid the groundwork for the modern-day Financial District and closed the book on the Revolutionary War.

Fraunces Tavern was once the fashionable place for polite gentlemen to dine. And on Evacuation Day in 1783, when British soldiers finally left America, it was in this windowed Long Room that General George Washington bade farewell to his officers. The toast marked a heartfelt end to the Revolutionary War and the start of American self-governance. You can imagine the long, wooden tables overflowing with food and tankards of ale, the worn Windsor chairs populated with celebratory generals.

The Long Room is just one of the highlights at this museum devoted to Colonial America. Visit the stylish Federalist dining room, where the wallpaper tells a story. One of only 11 surviving examples of this pattern by Zuber, the venerable French wallpaper company, the 1838 hand block print begins with a standard landscape that is lush and colorful. Then the client chose what other imagery they wished to be added to the foreground. Here you will see figures from the Revolutionary War. So prized are these personalized wallpapers that Jackie Kennedy added a Zuber set to the White House in 1961.

Other objects offer simple delights, like the diminutive, gold silk slipper worn by Martha Washington. Spot-lit in its own glass case, the pointed toe and rhinestone buckle seem fashion-forward. Nearby, a suite of early American flags line a double-height brick wall. You will notice how the design and colors for the flag developed over time on the State, Union, and French Regiment examples. Then for some early American fun, you can don one of the Revolutionary War costumes on hand, and pose in front of a vintage flag for a colonial-style selfie.

Address 54 Pearl Street, New York, NY 10004, +1 (212)425-1778, www.frauncestavernmuseum.org, info@frauncestavernmuseum.org | **Getting there** Subway to Whitehall Street/South Ferry (R, W), Bowling Green (4, 5), South Ferry (1), Broad Street (J, Z) | **Hours** Mon–Fri noon–5pm, Sat & Sun 11am–5pm | **Tip** Across the street, see the Portal Down to Old New York, an excavated section of the sidewalk, covered in thick glass, that shows preserved remnants of the Lovelace Tavern, which stood there in 1670. It's one time in New York when you should look down instead of up (63 Pearl Street, New York, NY 10004).

# 31__The Frick Collection

*So very romantic*

Even among the world-class museums in New York City, the Frick Collection is a rare jewel of exceptional beauty. Built by industrialist Henry Clay Frick (1849–1919), it was once a lavish home that has been turned into a museum. Visitors feel like guests as they take in masterpiece paintings, sculptures, and decorative arts. But it is the beloved Fragonard Room that may well be the most romantic room in the city. And the fascinating story behind it is a tale of love, rejection, and rebuilding.

It all began with a mistress. Comtesse du Barry, the lover of French King Louis XV, was building a pleasure pavilion near Paris. In 1771, she asked Jean-Honoré Fragonard to paint four canvases depicting the stages of love: the pursuit, a secret meeting, marriage, and reading love letters. The towering canvases are filled with glorious gardens, frothy brushwork, and courtly love. They are exceedingly romantic, and yet the Comtesse wasn't pleased. She refused the paintings and returned them to Fragonard. Years later, the artist installed them in his cousin's villa in southern France, and he painted seven additional canvases. The works remained there for some 100 years, until American banker J.P. Morgan purchased the paintings for his London townhouse. But when Morgan died, Frick saw an opportunity. In 1915, he bought the entire suite. Even though Frick had just moved into his mansion, he had his new drawing room reconfigured to make room for the paintings. Special wood paneling, or *boiserie,* was made in France to frame the paintings perfectly. Textiles from an iconic French fabric maker adorn the windows. Even exquisite hardware graces the doors.

A century later, the Fragonard Room remains a treasure in the history of art. Surrounded by exquisite furniture and porcelain, it's a pastel nod to 18th-century France – and a bold tribute to love and opportunity.

**Address** 1 East 70th Street, New York, NY 10021, +1 (212)288-0700, www.frick.org, info@frick.org | **Getting there** Subway to 68th Street (6), Lexington Avenue/ 63rd Street (F, N, Q), 72nd Street (Q) | **Hours** Tue–Sat 10am–6pm, Sun 11am–5pm | **Tip** Indulge in a bit of culinary romance with the pastel-colored macaroons at Ladurée, a taste of Paris on the Upper East Side (864 Madison Avenue, New York, NY 10021, www.laduree.fr/en/laduree-new-york).

# 32__Gracie Mansion
*Inside the little White House*

A visit to Gracie Mansion, surrounded by trees at the northern end of the East River, is like escaping to the country – only it's right on the Upper East Side. The 1799 Federal-style home is the official residence for the Mayor of New York City. Most people don't realize they can enjoy private tours here and a chance to see how New York's first families live.

Built as a private home for Scottish-born merchant Archibald Gracie, this mansion was a quiet escape from the frenetic streets of Lower Manhattan and hosted guests like Alexander Hamilton and John Quincy Adams. After many different lives, it was turned into the mayoral residence in 1942, and since then, each mayor has left his mark.

In the 1980s, Mayor Edward Koch was determined to bring the mansion back to its Federal-style roots. He visited the White House and was smitten with the Zuber wallpaper Jackie Kennedy had added (see ch. 30). Miraculously, a similar 1830 Zuber wallpaper was discovered in its original packaging in the attic of a home in upstate New York. It was installed in the mansion's dining room and still dazzles today.

In 2002, Major Michael Bloomberg preferred to live in his own townhouse, but he oversaw a major renovation of Gracie Mansion. The black-and-white floor in the foyer only looks like marble. It was painted to look like stone in the 1800s and then restored in recent years by New York City artisans living with HIV.

Nowhere are the layers of history more prominent than in the ballroom, where a period fireplace was added in 1966. The mantle's actual story goes back to 1804, when Alexander Hamilton was shot in a duel. The founding father was brought to his friend's house in Greenwich Village, where he died the next day – in front of this same fireplace. Finally, watch out for the spirit of Elizabeth Wolcott-Gracie, who died here in 1819. She is known to make appearances.

Address East 88th Street & East End Avenue, New York, NY 10028, +1 (212)676-3060, www1.nyc.gov/site/gracie/visit/visit.page, gracieinfo@cityhall.nyc.gov | Getting there Subway to 86th Street (4, 5, 6), 86th Street and Second Avenue (Q) | Hours See website to book a tour | Tip The mansion is located inside Carl Schurz Park along the East River, where you can stroll on the beautiful waterfront promenade and enjoy the views of Roosevelt and Randalls and Wards Islands (www.nycgovparks.org/parks/carl-schurz-park).

# 33_ Green-Wood Cemetery Gate House

*Drop dead gorgeous*

Green-Wood Cemetery is one of the most beautifully landscaped places in New York City. Curving roads wind up hills and past elaborate tombs, statues, and mausoleums. "This was New York's first museum," manager of programs Harry Weil says. "People would come here to see the sculpture long before the Met was established." Indeed, this was the Victorian hot spot to picnic and socialize, a public park before there were public parks.

That sense of discovery continues today at the cemetery's Gate House, a tiny museum inside a miniature Victorian cottage with mosaic floors and stained-glass windows. This is where visitors would rest after the long journey to get here. And today this teeny tiny jewel box space hosts the most intriguing exhibits of life and death.

Cherished pieces from Brooklyn's former Morbid Anatomy Museum have been on view here. Curious objects of death and mourning. Apocalyptic paintings and ceramic funeral crowns. Even engraved, silver coffin plates; "This one says 'We Miss You At Home'," Weil reads aloud, "How crushing is that?" Other exhibitions have featured the cemetery's own collection of art; some 400 pieces once owned, or painted by, people buried here: "We refer to those pieces as 'works by our permanent residents'," Weil muses. Highlights of that collection were hung salon style inside the handsome Gate House. Then visitors had maps to explore Green-Wood on their own; a cemetery art treasure hunt of sorts.

Don't miss French artist Sophie Calle's site-specific art installation, *Here Lie the Secrets of The Visitors of Green-Wood Cemetery*, where you can scribble your most intimate secrets onto papers, and lay them to rest inside a grave designed by the artist. Try to time your visit with one of their Twilight Tours.

Address 500 25th Street, Brooklyn, NY 11232, +1 (718)768-7300, www.green-wood.com, info@green-wood.com | Getting there Subway to 25th Street (R), 36th Street (D, F, N) | Hours Daily, Oct–Mar 8am–5pm, Apr–Sept 7am–7pm; see website for Gate House exhibition dates and times | Tip Knock the pins down at Melody Lanes Bowling Center, with its nostalgic bar and vintage neon decor – it's old-school Brooklyn cool (461 37th Street, Brooklyn, NY 11232, www.melodylanesny.com).

# 34 Grolier Club
*A bibliophile's paradise*

Books, in and of themselves, can be beautiful. This is just one of the guiding principles behind the grand Grolier Club, where the book arts are celebrated in the greatest of style. Just steps from Barney's Department Store and the shopping frenzy on Madison Avenue, you'll find quiet repose inside this discrete townhouse. "The most surprising thing about the Grolier Club for first-time visitors, is that we are open to the public and free," says Director Eric Holzenberg. Lucky for us.

Step through the brass-trimmed front doors and escape into a most rarified Upper East Side world. The handsome oil painting in the foyer is a portrait of book lover extraordinaire Robert Hoe, who started the club in 1884. He and his colleagues named it after the famed French bibliophile Jean Grolier (1489–1565). It's been going strong ever since.

Several galleries here feature delights, and anything they are showing is worth seeing. The appeal is partly the space itself. With its Chippendale-style chairs, handsome woodwork, and worn, oriental carpets, the mood is genteel and smart. Rotating exhibitions feature books as objects of artistic and historical interest. It's not only what the book is about, but also how it's made – the cover, bindings, typography, and illustrations. Topics range from flowers to chess, calligraphy to war. Authors like Sylvia Plath might be featured, along with Japanese prints or art nouveau posters. The range of exhibits is inspiring.

And in this digital age, it's nice to know the Grolier Club is busier than ever with its 100,000-volume library. "The physical, printed book remains an important, beautiful, and historically significant object," Holzenberg says. And here you'll find the sense of old New York flavored for the modern age. The faster we live, the more we seek out quiet places to slow down. This club is a busy New Yorker's dream come true.

**Address** 47 East 60th Street, New York, NY 10022, +1 (212)838-6690, www.grolierclub.org | **Getting there** Subway to Fifth Avenue/60th Street (N, R, W), 59th Street/Lexington Avenue (4, 5, 6), Lexington Avenue/63rd Street (F) | **Hours** Mon–Sat 10am–5pm | **Tip** Stop by for a cocktail at the iconic Monkey Bar, with its massive Ed Sorel mural depicting sixty Jazz Age icons like Billie Holiday (60 East 54th Street, New York, NY 10022, www.monkeybarnewyork.com).

# 35 Gulliver's Gate

*Lilliputians in Times Square*

Right in the chaos that is Times Square, you'll find a hidden museum where miniatures are turned into magic. With thousands of teeny-tiny buildings, bridges, people, and cars, Gulliver's Gate is a fascinating micro world, the width of an entire city block. Up the escalator to the second floor, you'll travel to Europe, Asia, Africa, North America, Latin America, and the Middle East. Highly detailed dioramas have interactive elements that are both witty and wonderful.

First stop: the Big Apple, only bite sized. See perfectly scaled, tiny versions of the Brooklyn Bridge, Empire State Building, Winter Garden Atrium, and Whitney Museum. Even Grand Central is filled with hordes of micro people. Look very closely, and you'll see little surprises too. A tiny woman has dropped her purse on the subway track. See Spider Man on the Brooklyn Bridge and Slimer from *Ghostbusters* on a street corner. You receive a special key with admission. Insert it in the little kiosks throughout to animate the scenes. The Macy's Thanksgiving Day Parade starts to move down the avenue, complete with miniature balloons floating in the air.

Wind your way along and you're in Greece, with a mini Parthenon and a Mount Olympus, where Zeus comes to life. In Italy there's the Grand Canal along Piazza San Marco. And in Scotland, a miniature Loch Ness Monster comes right out of the water. Especially beautiful are the tiny Taj Mahal in India and snow-covered Red Square in Moscow. You'll soon be planning your next trip, in real size.

Throughout the museum are working ateliers where model makers continuously create new pieces. If you want to be a part of the fun, step into the 3-D scanner, which will record your exact likeness. For around $50 they'll make a tiny likeness of you called a Model Citizen. You decide in which vignette they place mini you. Stonehenge is a popular choice.

Address 216 West 44th Street, New York, NY 10036, +1 (212)235-2016, www.gulliversgate.com | Getting there Subway to 42nd Street/Port Authority (A, C, E, N, Q, R, W, 1, 2, 3), 42nd Street/Bryant Park (B, D, F, M) | Hours Daily 10am–8pm | Tip Have a drink at the iconic Sardi's Restaurant, where hundreds of caricatures of theater celebrities line the walls. See how many you recognize (234 West 44th Street, New York, NY 100036, www.sardis.com).

# 36  Hamilton Grange

*A life in the country*

When Alexander Hamilton was building his 1802 dream house in Harlem, he wanted it to be grand, but not too grand. By now he was as a seasoned statesman. And this "sweet project," as he called it, would be the culmination of an extraordinary life. What makes it all the more poignant is that the founding father only lived here for two years before he died.

You can visit Hamilton Grange today, tucked into a tidy park on 141st Street. It is surrounded by brownstones, bus stops, and a funeral parlor. But back in his day, this area was the countryside. There were apple orchards, fields of clover, and views of both the Hudson and East Rivers. It was bucolic. Yet even though it was Hamilton who founded the nation's financial system, this ambitious project left him deeply in debt.

Step into the diminutive library off the entryway, and you feel the spirit of the man at his simple wooden desk adorned with a quill pen. The striking apple-green wall color is thought to be the original, based on analysis of the room's many paint layers. Green was an expensive pigment at the time, often reserved for smaller rooms like this. Next door, the mood softens in the yellow-walled, octagonal-shaped dining room, where the three large windows would be flung open during dinner parties. And outside, amidst the flower gardens, musicians would softly serenade the guests.

Sadly, Hamilton's later years were filled with tragedy. In 1801, his son Philip died in a duel defending his father's honor. Daughter Angelica suffered a mental breakdown. And on July 11, 1804, the most famous duel in America took place between Hamilton and Vice President Aaron Burr. Standing 10 paces apart, both men fired, and Hamilton fell to the ground, mortally wounded. He survived one more day, long enough to see his wife and children. But with a single bullet, his dream of a life in the country was over.

Address 414 West 141st Street, New York, NY 10031, +1 (646)548-2310, www.nps.gov.com | Getting there Subway to West 137th Street (1), West 145th Street (A, B, C, D) | Hours Wed–Sun 9am–5pm | Tip See another historic house museum nearby, the Morris-Jumel Mansion. Built in 1765, it's one of the city's oldest residences, with lovely views of both the Hudson and Harlem Rivers (65 Jumel Terrace, New York, NY 10032, www.morrisjumel.org).

# 37 Harbor Defense Museum

*From cannons to camouflage*

It takes a bit of maneuvering just to pass through the strict security at this hidden museum located right on the Fort Hamilton Army base in Bay Ridge, Brooklyn. You pass through checkpoints, show IDs, and fill out paperwork if parking a car. Then find your way to a brick-walled, 19th-century caponier, home of the Harbor Defense Museum, where the story of protecting New York's Harbor is told in lively fashion.

"We have people on the base who don't know we are here," says museum guide Bob Bruina. "We're the best-kept secret." Begin with the expertly tailored military uniforms from the American Revolutionary War. These recreations of the originals show pure innovation of design. We see a Delaware Regiment Continental Army blue jacket with red facing and a white waistcoat. The buttoned back coat lapels could be secured together in cold weather. Handsome in both form and function. "Soldiers wore bright uniforms so they could see each other on the battlefield," Bruina says, "but they also made them targets." That's the story of the development of camouflage uniforms in years to come.

The museum focuses a great deal on weaponry used to protect the harbor from invasion. See the very tall and slender Brown Bess Musket, used during the American Revolutionary War. Its razor sharp bayonet looks particularly menacing. Then we see the carronade cannon from 1810, designed to provide ships with devastating firepower at close range. There are sabers, World War I rifles, and machine guns on display. Even a massive, Flank Howitzer cannon weighing 1,400 pounds. Dating from 1864, it shot out 48 separate iron balls at one time.

You will also see a building fragment from the World Trade Center, recovered after the September 11, 2001 terrorist attack. Members of the army here were deployed to Ground Zero, where they manned a hospital, a poignant symbol of the modern-day military.

Address 230 Sheridan Loop, Brooklyn, NY 11252, +1 (718)630-4349, www.harbor-defense-museum.business.site | Getting there Subway to Bay Ridge/95th Street (R) | Hours Mon–Fri 10am–4pm | Tip Just across the Verrazano Bridge, visit another historic military site, Fort Wadsworth, now a public park with beautiful water views (210 New York Avenue, Staten Island, NY 10305, www.nps.gov/gate/learn/historyculture/fort-wadsworth).

# 38 Holographic Studios
*Into the depths of 3-D*

Taking a tour of the weird and wonderful Holographic Studios is like spending time with a quirky uncle. When you leave you're not quite sure what to make of the colorful visit. Dr. Laser, as he calls himself, enthusiastically greets you at the door. He wears a white lab coat with his moniker printed on the pocket. His real name is Jason Sapan, and he is the King of Holography, who has been running this gallery and studio since 1979.

Here against a craggy brick wall are plexiglass mounts holding random holographic wonders Sapan has created over the years. There's Andy Warhol reading a newspaper, as he slowly turns in his chair. Nearby you'll see a glowing image of Phil Donahue and a colorful portrait of Phyllis Diller, who seems to stare right at you. Sapan says this is the world's longest operating gallery of holography, and one of the few remaining outposts creating these 3-D works of art.

Next, the good doctor takes you through narrow hallways heaped with boxes, tools, and equipment; down to his tiny laser laboratory in a darkened subterranean basement. You wonder if you will ever be able to escape. He quickly lights a cigarette, fanning the smoke around his face. And then you see it! He shines a laser at the smoke, creating a sinuous, neon web. Like a mad scientist, he makes scary sound effects. Mesmerized by his colorful creation, you know you are not at the Met!

Part camp, part magician, Sapan shows a series of holograms he's made for clients like IBM and TAG Heuer, and even a music video for the 1980s band A Flock Of Seagulls. "I starred in that one," he reports. He's fond of referencing scary movies, while citing scientific facts: "A hologram the size of a human brain can hold every piece of written information ever recorded." Try and wrap your brain around that tidbit. There are many more wacky wonders hidden in this holographic haven.

Address 240 East 26th Street, New York, NY 10010, +1 (212)686-9397, www.holographer.com, holographylab@gmail.com | Getting there Subway to 23rd Street (6, N, R, W) | Hours Mon–Fri 2–6pm | Tip Nearby is Eataly, featuring specialties from all regions of Italy. You can buy food products to take home, or dine in their many restaurants, all under one roof – and one on the rooftop (200 Fifth Avenue, New York, NY 10010, www.eataly.com/us_en/stores/nyc-flatiron).

# 39__Houdini Museum

*Escapism at its best*

Not far from the Penn Station pandemonium, you'll find a secret museum devoted to magic. Walk through the eye-catching art deco office lobby, up to the fourth floor. Push open the glass door, and you've escaped into the world of Harry Houdini (1874–1926). Just like magic.

This red-walled, one-room museum is the personal indulgence of its wizard-like founder Roger Dreyer, who did magic tricks as a kid and never stopped. Houdini is his hero. and he's collected hundreds of props, posters, and personal items from the great escapist. In the corner sits a padlocked, vintage steamer trunk wrapped in heavy chains. It was part of Houdini's famous Metamorphosis, a feat of illusion and escape. Nearby, a 1907 wooden coffin looks menacing. Houdini escaped from it, even though the lid was heavily nailed down.

Because he was known as Harry 'Handcuff' Houdini, several metal handcuffs are on display, along with tiny keys or metal devices, which the master hid on his body or swallowed and then surreptitiously used later on. You'll surely notice a glass frame nearby, where The Punisher hangs against the wall. It's a canvas straightjacket from which the magician miraculously escaped. Perfectly frightening. And finally, all around the room, there are Houdini-related advertisements, letters, and documents, which illustrate his extraordinary life. We forget that Houdini became a motion picture star in the early days of film, and here we see images of the handsome illusionist, looking every bit the movie star.

If you want to try some magic yourself, you're in luck. Right inside the museum is the Fantasma Magic Shop, where you can buy trick cards, wands, and vanishing silks. They often demonstrate some of the magic tricks for customers, and everyone is encouraged to participate and enjoy. You'll feel like part of the club in this mystifying magic hideaway.

Address 213 West 35th Street, Suite 401, New York, NY 10001, +1 (212)244-3633, www.houdinimuseumny.com | Getting there Subway to 34th Street/Penn Station (1, 2, 3, A, C, E) | Hours Mon–Fri 10am–6pm, Sat & Sun 10am–5pm | Tip If you are a fan of *Project Runway*, the massive Mood fabric store featured on the show is nearby. The vast variety of fabrics is impressive, even if you can't sew a stitch (225 West 37th Street, New York, NY 10018, www.moodfabrics.com).

# 40 International Center of Photography

*Capturing the decisive moments*

At a time when nearly everyone is capturing images of daily life and sending the photos out into the world, how do photography curators decide which images are significant and worth saving? That's the very modern mission of the International Center of Photography, where the visual past, present, and future meld into one.

Situated on the newly hip Bowery in Lower Manhattan, broad storefront windows along the street welcome visitors into an engaging public space. Come and ponder the ways images shape our world.

Started in 1974 by Cornell Capa, ICP was set up by photographers for photographers. At its core is preserving the works of Magnum, an iconic collection of independent photojournalists, documenting the world post-World War II. Thousands of their works fill the archives. And so do a growing number of contemporary images that go beyond photos framed on a wall. Exhibitions here might offer video-based, wall-sized projections; visual recruiting material from ISIS; or fast-paced GoPro videos of extreme sports. Curators try to hold a mirror up to an ever-changing visual landscape through workshops, tours, and talks. A comprehensive school is affiliated with the center, where dozens of classes shape future photographers.

Still, the history of photography will always be present here, and the intimate galleries, with low ceilings, invite quiet contemplation. Examples might include the poignant 1960s photos by Danny Lyon who documented inmates at a Texas prison. Or the heart-stopping 1970s images of an Italian psychiatric hospital, photographed by Raymond Depardon. They are brief snippets of our complicated world, captured in still moments. Up close these black-and-white photos hold great power. It's a dance the ICP does so well: showing visual images that gracefully glide somewhere between art and documentation of life.

Address 250 Bowery, New York, NY 10012, +1 (212)857-0000, www.icp.org,
info@icp.org | Getting there Subway to 2nd Avenue (F), Broadway/Lafayette (B, D,
F, M, 6), Bowery (J, Z), Prince Street (N, R) | Hours Tue–Wed, Fri–Sun 10am–6pm,
Thu 10am–9pm | Tip For a rustic and groovy tavern, have a bite at Freemans, a
restaurant at the end of one of Manhattan's few alleyways (Freeman Alley, New York,
NY 10002, www.freemansrestaurant.com).

# 41 International Print Center

*Creating new masters of an ancient art form*

Right in the heart of the buzzy Chelsea Gallery scene, you'll find a small exhibition space devoted to the power of the print. But beware – this is not a dusty old etchings collection. Part of the joy of visiting the International Print Center is the space itself, where a wall of windows hover above the High Line, perfectly framing the city skyline beyond. Enter the lobby of this industrial-tinged building, where an elevator operator is on hand to take you to the fifth floor. The ride is vintage New York.

"Printing here is very broadly defined," director Judy Hecker says. "It could be a floor installation, a wall stencil, a video animation, or a printed zine." You feel that spirit of experimentation with their ongoing New Prints Program, where artists from all over the world submit work from the past 12 months. The selected pieces show printmakers pushing the limits at a specific moment in time. There are digital print transfers on broken pieces of porcelain, and even a screen print on a small chunk of ice; as it melts, a video records the ephemeral nature of the work.

Rotating exhibitions feature linocuts, woodcuts, aquatints, and screen prints, a wide range of techniques that show this evolving art form. The exhibition Black Pulp offered perspectives on black identity in American culture with contemporary works shown alongside rare historical books, comics, newspapers, and related ephemera. "It's a new visual vocabulary," Hecker says. "People realize printing is not just a small Rembrandt etching, it is also very relevant to today."

If you are curious about how prints are actually made, there is a small workshop inside the gallery, where artists in residence are making works right before your eyes. Then, for the ultimate hands-on experience, come for one of their drop-in days, where you may get to make a print yourself and take it home.

Address 508 West 26th Street, 5th floor, New York, NY 10001, +1 (212)989-5090, www.ipcny.org, contact@ipcny.org | Getting there Subway to 23rd Street (C, E), 34th/11th Avenue (7) | Hours Tue – Sat 11am – 6pm | Tip Visit Gagosian Gallery, a leading gallery of the art world, where super sleek, cavernous galleries show today's top artists (555 West 24th Street, New York, NY 10011, www.gagosian.com).

# 42 Japan Society

*A tranquil escape*

Around the United Nations buildings, there's an air of worldliness to this little pocket of New York City. Foreign flags flutter, snippets of unknown languages float by. And yet in the midst of this international swirl, one landmarked building stands out. Is it modern or traditional? Far Eastern or Upper East Side? Maybe a blending of both.

That was the idea back in 1971, when Japanese architect Junzō Yoshimura set out to design a new home for the Japan Society. He infused the low-slung building with the strict lines of modernist architecture, but then softened it with a Japanese aesthetic, creating an intriguing yin and yang. Step inside the lobby, and you've escaped into another realm. Wooden slats line the low ceiling, allowing warm light to filter into the space. Bamboo trees bring texture, and a water feature softly bubbles. You are at peace.

It's the perfect backdrop to take in their artfully curated exhibitions in the second-floor galleries. This isn't the place for big blockbuster exhibits. They are more likely to be well-considered, one-of-a-kind offerings that make you supremely glad you made the effort to come here.

Past exhibitions have included the monumental, black-and-white photos of acclaimed contemporary Japanese photographer Hiroshi Sugimoto, who illustrated a little known 16th-century encounter between Japan and the West. Or the vibrantly painted screens and scrolls, by 16th-century master Hasegawa Tōhaku. For this exhibit, visitors were seated before the screens and experienced how the artworks would have been shown on the floor of a temple, lit by candlelight. Other topics include Buddhist sculpture, calligraphy, ceramics, and samurai swords. Two to three exhibitions are mounted each year. The society also hosts an active film society, with year-round screenings of favorite classics and recent discoveries in new Japanese cinema.

Address 333 East 47th Street, New York, NY 10017, +1 (212)832-1155,
www.japansociety.org | Getting there Subway to Grand Central/42nd Street (4, 5,
6, 7, S), 53rd Street/Lexington Avenue (E, M) | Hours Tue–Thu noon–7pm, Fri
noon–9pm, Sat & Sun 11am–5pm; check website for class schedule | Tip Hobnob
with the diplomatic crowd from across the street at the internationally posh World Bar
(845 United Nations Plaza, New York, NY 10017, www.hospitatilyholdings.com).

# 43___Jewish Museum

*Scenes from the collection*

The Jewish Museum is never dull. Housed in a 1908 French-chateau-style building on the Upper East Side, the museum mounts some of the best exhibitions in the city. From portraits by Modigliani to fashions by Isaac Mizrahi, themes touch on Jewish culture but are thoughtfully curated for all. And now, there is something new. "Scenes from the Collection" transforms the entire third floor with nearly 600 works. Featuring antiquities and contemporary art, the exhibits offer a varied mix in a modern way to showcase the collection, broken into scenes, much like a movie. Some treasures are on view for the very first time.

Personas is one such scene. It explores the layered idea of portraiture. Here you'll see multiple self-portraits by stalwarts such as Louise Nevelson, Cindy Sherman, Man Ray, and Lee Krasner, each a marvel on its own. Then, in a year or so, curators will add new works to the mix to keep the offerings fresh.

Next up: Taxonomies. Ready yourself for the tiny, shocking-pink closet of a room that channels the Renaissance Cabinet of Wonders. Jam-packed with dozens and dozens of small treasures, it's a visual tableau that feels like a mini museum, with jewel-encrusted Torah crowns, spice containers, watches, tools, and tiny sailing ships. There is even a model of the ancient Temple of Jerusalem – in a bottle. Fascinating. Then nearby, you'll find vintage stereoscopes, or hand-held viewers, that allow you to look at double photographs. Magically, the images seem 3-D, with a visual slight of hand.

Finally, a small viewing area off to the side features snippets from various television shows that highlight Jewish life and culture. Scenes from programs like *Orange is the New Black* or *Grace and Frankie* offer clips that are both poignant and chuckle worthy. In this museum, amidst the galleries filled with glorious objects, is a modern take on Jewish culture.

Address 1109 5th Avenue, New York, NY 10128, +1 (212)432-3200, www.thejewishmuseum.org, info@jm.org | Getting there Subway 86th Street (4, 5, 6) | Hours Fri–Tue, Sat 11am–5:45pm, Thu 11am–8pm | Tip For some of the city's best talks, readings, and concerts, head to the 92nd Street Y, a cultural center where guests like Tom Ford, Billy Joel, and Jon Stewart have all graced the stage (1395 Lexington Avenue, New York, NY 10128, www92y.org).

# 44 Leslie-Lohman Museum

*Pushing the boundaries of gay and lesbian art*

Tucked alongside a cobbled street in SoHo, the brick building with its stately row of Corinthian columns is vintage New York City. But the museum inside has a very modern mission to collect, preserve, and show the works of LGBTQ artists. It all started in the 1960s, when life partners Charles W. Leslie and Fritz Lohman decided to open an art gallery in SoHo. The idea was to provide a sanctuary where gay artists could show their work. The gallery eventually morphed into an accredited museum in 2011, and now it's the only museum in the world devoted completely to gay and lesbian art as a cultural center for LGBTQ community, scholarship, and creativity.

Housed in a recently renovated space, the tall storefront windows and soaring ceilings bring light into airy galleries in which you can view paintings, sculptures, videos, and interactive installations. Once an underground movement dealing mostly with male, homoerotic art, today LGBTQ art has blossomed into a varied and visibly strong political force. Women artists now play a key role, as do artists who are transsexual and of diverse cultural backgrounds.

Exhibitions rotate, and the curators often pull from the museum's extensive permanent collection. Key works might include the compelling black-and-white photos of Robert Mapplethorpe, or the colorful imagery of Keith Haring. But there's often a sense of discovery as well, like the 2005 painting by artist Arthur Hammer, a portrait of two men, both wearing plaid shirts. Life partners since the 1960s, they sit side by side yet not touching, typical of gay couples of their generation when out in public.

More contemporary works might include a full-length, nude painting by artist Janet Bruesselbach. In *A Lady Betwixt (Robin)* (2015), we see one of her many large-scale portraits portraying trans women. Painted in a classical vein, it pushes historic figurative themes. It is just one of the many works here that challenges the norm.

Address 26 Wooster Street, New York, NY 10013, +1 (212)431-2609, www.leslielohman.org, info@leslielohman.org | Getting there Subway to Canal Street (1, A, C, E, N, R, W) | Hours Wed–Sun noon–6pm, Thu noon–8pm | Tip The atmospheric SoHo Art Materials is an old-fashioned art supply store filled with cool notebooks, pens, and papers for when inspiration hits you (7 Wooster Street, New York, NY 10013, www.sohoartmaterials.com).

# 45 Lewis H. Latimer House

*A lifetime of light bulb moments*

Step inside the mind of a true Renaissance man with a trip to this charming Queen Anne-style cottage – in Queens. African-American inventor and electrical pioneer Lewis H. Latimer lived here from 1903 until his death in 1928. The tiny rooms of this clapboard home are filled with patent documents, technical drawings, artworks, and poems, all evidence of an overlooked genius who was the ultimate self-made man.

Glowing, vintage light fixtures here take on added meaning because it was Latimer who helped usher in the age of electric light. He was the right-hand man for Thomas Edison, inventor of the light bulb. But Latimer vastly improved the bulb by inventing and patenting the carbon filament, which made the bulb burn much longer. Latimer also played a critical role in the development of the telephone while working for Alexander Graham Bell. He was instrumental in establishing street lighting in America, along with the construction of electric plants in London and Montreal. All of this from an entirely self-educated man, the son of fugitive slaves who first taught himself mechanical drawing while in the Navy.

From room to room, the sunny yellow walls and Victorian furniture highlight the domestic side of Lewis Latimer, who was also an artist and a poet. A framed pastel portrait he created of his daughter appears warm and tender. An antique hutch holds his poetry books, a passion he indulged in during his later years. You feel a palpable connection to this remarkable man, who hatched very big ideas while living in this small home.

Finally, the delightfully named "Tinker Lab," keeps the spirit of discovery alive for children. Here they take part in hands-on workshops where little ones can make things and fiddle with a variety of materials. The focus is often on technology and building the next generation of inventors for the 21st century.

Address 34-41 137th Street, Flushing, NY 11354, +1 (718)961-8585, www.latimernow.org, lewislatimerhouse@gmail.com | Getting there Subway to Main Street Roosevelt (7); bus to Linden Place and 35th Avenue (Q25) | Hours Wed, Fri, Sun noon–5pm | Tip Visit the surprising and grand Ganesh Temple, home to the Hindu Temple Society of North America. Stay for a delicious lunch of South Asian dishes at the Temple Canteen (45-57 Bowne Street, Flushing, NY 11355, www.nyganeshtemple.org).

# 46 Living Museum

*An art asylum*

In all of New York City, perhaps the museum that is most filled with life is found at the Creedmoor Psychiatric Hospital in Queens. The aptly named Living Museum is itself a conceptual work of art, a place where, for 35 years, the patients have been expressing themselves through art. "People don't realize that mentally ill people can be very creative," program director Dr. Janos Marton says. "What we offer here is a protected environment."

Visitors are allowed in by special appointment only. Located inside the former Creedmoor kitchen hall, the museum's floors are cement. A chain-link fence surrounds a second-floor walkway. Inpatients, outpatients, and counselors work inside the giant studio, where tables are heaped with papers, palettes, yarn, metal wire, fabric, frames, and brushes. There are paintings of superheroes, crucifixes, and teddy bears. It does not feel like a locked psychiatric ward, but more like an art collective. You see work being made on the spot, while all around, sculptures, drawings, and paintings are on display. The dense layers of art created here over the years are a living archive of unfiltered creativity.

At one time, Creedmoor housed up to 7,000 patients. But with improved medications and a move away from such institutions, that number is now around 300. Most of the artists are outpatients. Some come daily, others weekly. "There are no rules here. People are simply free to create," Marton explains.

Moving through, you are struck by the sense of wit. A vintage suitcase-turned-sculpture is wryly painted *Creedmoor Grounds, Resident Genius*. An entire wall of defunct 1960s television sets reads, *Pain, The Only Proof of Reality*. Some works are joyous, others intense. But everywhere, there is a sense of immediacy and of life because as Dr. Marton explains, the guiding principle here is to use "vulnerability as a weapon."

Address 80-45 Winchester Boulevard, Queens Village, NY 11427, +1 (718)264-3490, www.omh.ny.gov/omhweb/facilities/crpc/visitor_guide.htm | Getting there Bus to Union Turnpike/Winchester Boulevard (QM 6) | Hours By appointment only, call for a private tour | Tip Spend time at a real farm, working since 1697, right in the city at the Queens County Farm Museum, where you can commune with cows, goats, and pigs (75-50 Little Neck Parkway, Queens, NY 11004, www.queensfarm.org).

# 47 Living Torah Museum

*Ancient history that's hands on*

Most museums have signs reading, *Do Not Touch*. Precious objects are displayed behind protective glass. But at this off-the-radar collection in Borough Park, touching priceless objects is encouraged. In fact, it's the guiding principle behind one of the most unique, innovative, and memorable museums in New York, a secret place worth discovering.

"If you feel and touch history, you know history," says museum guide and curator Rabbi Deutsch, who oversees this assemblage of hundreds of objects, all mentioned in the Torah or Bible. Through hands-on contact with ancient artifacts, history comes alive.

Part magician, part scholarly raconteur, Rabbi Deutsch leads small, private groups of all denominations through the antiquities room, where you can actually hold in your hand a paper-thin, 24-carat gold crown. It is 2,500 years old. Feel free to touch a silver coin dating back to Alexander the Great, or try on a weighty, bronze Illyrian helmet from ancient Greece. You'll see gold rings and earrings from ancient Egypt, intricate marvels placed right in your palm. Rarely is this type of hands-on learning allowed. History never felt so intimate.

Next, you'll climb a steep staircase into a most rarified menagerie: a startling, cover-every-inch room filled with a dizzying assortment of taxidermy specimens featured in ancient texts – stuffed zebras, snakes, and birds. Here you can stroke the head of a lion, feel the silky coat of a fox, or caress the scaly skin of a cobra. Only animals that have died naturally are part of the collection, and up-close, this private co-mingling with the animal kingdom is riveting. Located in a modest residential duplex, this no-frills, vintage space feels old-school Borough Park. That's part of the charm. But it somehow feels modern too, with its immersive approach to learning, where multi-sensory education is the wave of the future.

Address 1601 41st Street, Brooklyn, NY 11218, +1 (718)851-3215, www.torahmuseum.com, info@torahmuseum.com | Getting there Subway to Ditmas Avenue (F); bus to McDonald Avenue/Cortelyou Road (B 67, B 69), 13th Avenue/41st Street (B 16) | Hours By appointment only, call to schedule a visit | Tip Put your striped conductor hat on and head to Trainworld, a vintage emporium filled with model trains, tracks, and tiny buildings, fittingly located right under the F train platform (751 McDonald Avenue, Brooklyn, NY 11218, www.trainworld.com).

# 48__Merchant's House

*Ghostly extravagance in the Village*

Sometimes historic house museums can be a little heavy, with cramped rooms densely packed with dark furniture. But the Merchant's House Museum focuses both on the people who lived there and their lifestyle. The experience here makes formal, 19th-century living fascinating. And when you leave, you understand history on a human level.

The wealthy, merchant-class Tredwell family (Seabury, Eliza, and their eight children) lived in this brick townhouse for nearly 100 years (1835–1933). Most of their furniture, clothing, and personal objects have remained. It's as if they might return at any moment. Rumored to be one of the most haunted houses in the city, the museum offers candlelight tours about family members who died here and the strange occurences that have taken place. Around Halloween, Victorian mourning customs are on exhibit, with a flower-topped casket in the parlor, where family funerals were actually held. Also in October, the 1865 deathbed of Mr. Tredwell is recreated with a bearded mannequin lying in the red-curtained bed where the patriarch breathed his last breath.

At the Merchant's House Museum, the emphasis is on real, day-to-day Victorian life, customs, and rituals. The rooms and objects tell stories based on strong curatorial research. This concept comes alive on a culinary tour in the family's 1850s kitchen. Here we see what dishes were prepared, along with Victorian dining dos and don'ts. Likewise, a special 'backstairs' tour looks at the family's four Irish servants, who lived on the fourth floor – a true immigrants' tale.

But whenever you come, remember to keep an eye out for ghostly signs of the youngest Tredwell daughter, Gertrude. Born here in 1840, she never married. She lived in this house until she died here at the age of 93. There have been reports by staff and visitors of strange sounds, scents, and sightings. You have been warned.

Address 29 East 4th Street, New York, NY 10003, +1 (212)777-1089, www.merchantshouse.org | Getting there Subway to 8th Street (N, R), Astor Place (6), Broadway/Lafayette (B, D, F, M) | Hours Thu noon–8pm, Fri–Mon noon–5pm | Tip Discover textiles, ceramics, and folk art at the Ukrainian Museum (222 East 6th Street, New York, NY 10003, www.ukranianmuseum.org).

# 49__ The Met Breuer

*Iconic design with a hidden surprise*

It's called brutalist architecture for a reason. With its brooding granite façade and fortress-like presence, this Madison Avenue building is either beloved or willfully ignored by New Yorkers. Designed in 1966 by Bauhaus architect Marcel Breuer, the Whitney Museum of American Art was located here for nearly 50 years. But the Whitney built a new home downtown, and in 2016, the Metropolitan Museum of Art moved in here, renaming it the Met Breuer (*BROY-er*). They present top notch modern and contemporary exhibitions and programming at this location, and it's been a perfect match.

Look up as you walk into the lobby. There are rows and rows of ceiling lights capped with moonlike shades. Hypnotic. Everything is a grayish-brown stone or concrete. Windows are asymmetrical. Exhibitions rotate and might include Diane Arbus photos, Edvard Munch paintings, or a survey of unfinished artworks. Always a compelling mix.

And yet, despite the change, there is one artwork that stayed in place, not in a gallery, but hidden in a stairwell between the first and second floors. There it is, positioned above a window: a cluster of clay mounds with miniature, seemingly abandoned, tiny buildings perched on top. Created by Charles Simonds in 1981, it's one of his "Dwellings" for what he calls an imaginary civilization of Little People. Look out the window across the street to the Apple Store on Madison Avenue, and you'll see another Dwelling tucked on the second-floor windowsill. A third Dwelling is on that building's chimney. All three are part of the same commission, meant to shift art out of the museum space. By placing the three clusters near one another, there is the sense of both habitation and abandonment. Over the past four decades, Simonds has built dozens of these curious structures in cities all over the world. They are wondrous to see – if you know where to look.

Address 945 Madison Avenue, New York, NY 10021, +1 (212)731-1675, www.metmuseum.org/visit/met-breuer, info@metmuseum.org | Getting there Subway to 77th Street (6); bus to 75th Street (M1, M2, M3, M4), Madison Avenue (M79) | Hours Tue–Thu 10am–5:30pm, Fri & Sat 10am–9pm, Sun 10am–5:30pm | Tip Keep the art theme going with a visit to Lévy Gorvy Gallery. The light-filled space shows some of the city's best art offerings (909 Madison Avenue, New York, NY 10021, www.levygorvy.com).

# 50___The Met Cloisters

*An unsolved medieval mystery*

Surely the most atmospheric museum in the city is the Cloisters. Perched high on a hill overlooking the Hudson River, the museum immerses you in medieval art, architecture, and gardens. And it's all real. The Gothic and Romanesque masonry was brought over from Europe to New York, where it would hold an extraordinary collection of illuminated manuscripts, stained glass, and sculpture. A visit to this museum transports you back to medieval times.

The magnificent *Unicorn Tapestries* are particularly astounding. Known as *The Hunt of the Unicorn*, the seven works are among the art world's greatest treasures. Because so little is known about them, they're among the most mysterious as well.

In their day, tapestries were prized possessions, more valuable than paintings or property. These works depict noblemen hunting for a white unicorn. But for whom were they made? Despite years of debate, experts don't know. The dress style suggests they were designed in France and produced in Belgium around 1500. The earliest record of the works is 1680, in the French castle of François VI de La Rochefoucauld. Adding further mystery, a cryptic clue is woven into each tapestry: the letters A and E bound together with a knotted rope. Does it symbolize a marriage? Adam and Eve?

The dazzling *Unicorn in Captivity* panel shows the white beast inside a low, circular fence. He is loosely tied to a pomegranate tree, which bears the red fruit often symbolizing fertility. You'll see red stains on the animal's white fur. It could be juice from the pomegranate tree, or perhaps blood, a reference to the Passion of Christ. Both secular and sacred theories persist, as scholars have been debating these ideas for more than a century. Finally, some 100 plants form the lush background, each with its own botanical symbolism. More clues? It's all part of this great medieval mystery, wrapped around a mythical animal, inside a magnificent cloister.

**Address** 99 Margaret Corbin Drive, New York, NY 10040, +1 (212)923-3700, www.metmuseum.org/visit/met-cloisters | **Getting there** Subway to 190th Street (A); bus to Margaret Corbin Drive/Cloisters (M4) | **Hours** Daily, Mar–Oct 10am–5:15pm, Nov–Feb 10am–4:45pm | **Tip** Nestled right inside the leafy Fort Tryon Park, the New Leaf restaurant lives up to its name with perfect views of the surrounding greenery. It was designed by the Olmsted Brothers and restored to its present beauty with the support of Bette Midler and the community (1 Margaret Corbin Drive, New York, NY 10040, www.newleafrestaurant.squarespace.com).

# 51 Metropolitan Museum of Art

*Big painting, little inaccuracies*

It's the grand, operatic star of the American Wing at the Metropolitan Museum of Art. Measuring a staggering 21-feet wide, *Washington Crossing the Delaware* depicts the surprise Christmas Day attack on Hessian soldiers that changed the course of the American Revolutionary War. Painted by German-American artist Emanuel Leutze in 1851, the nearly-life-sized General George Washington stands tall in the boat, gazing at the distant shore, while soldiers and horses jostle in icy waters.

Surprisingly, there are small historical inaccuracies imbedded in the composition that are intriguing to find when you take a closer look. The painting captures the 1776 crossing to Trenton, New Jersey in vivid daylight, but the event actually took place in the dark of night. Those wobbly, shallow boats could not have possibly held the horses and artillery, and they seem to be pointed in the wrong direction. The rippling American flag anchoring the composition had not yet been adopted.

Leutze actually painted the work in Düsseldorf, Germany, some 75 years after this famous scene. The artist hoped the painting would inspire European reformers. He grew up in America but later returned to Germany, and it is believed he used the River Rhine as a model for the rough ice chunks in the painting, which are far different from the flat sheets of ice commonly found on the Delaware River. Yet despite historical inaccuracies, the heroic painting caused a sensation when it was shown in America in 1851. Washington was a cult figure at the time, and this work mythologized him.

Examine the extraordinary gilt frame around the painting, itself a work of art. The original frame was lost, but this reproduction was made for the museum in 2011 from an historical photo.

Address 1000 5th Avenue, New York, NY 10028, +1 (212)535-7710, www.metmuseum.org |
Getting there Subway to 86th Street (4, 5, 6); bus to 82nd Street (M1, M2, M3, M4) |
Hours Sun–Thu 10am–5:30pm, Fri & Sat 10am–9pm | Tip Enjoy lunch at a classic Upper
East Side diner, Nectar, a perfect place for Madison Avenue people watching (1090 Madison
Avenue, New York, NY 10028, www.eatnectarnyc.com).

# 52 Mets Hall of Fame

*Meet the Mets!*

He is one of the most iconic mascots in all of sports history. And here he is, front and center, ready to greet you. He's the original Mr. Met, with his giant, baseball-shaped, papier-mâché head. First introduced on programs in 1963, he was turned into a live costumed character a year later. Replaced today by a felt version, the original is pure Mets nostalgia.

This is just one of the treasures awaiting discovery in this pixie-sized museum right inside Citi Field. Open during game days, this place is a Mets-fan wonderland. You'll see bright orange and blue seats from Shea Stadium, the Mets' home from 1964 to 2008. Then nearby, dainty looking metal chairs from the Polo Grounds, where the team played at the start of their franchise from 1962 to 1963. You'll see a rare, carved wood-and-brass ashtray in the shape of Shea Stadium, along with a ticket to the Mets' very first home game on April 13, 1962. A vintage bobblehead charms. A 1960s record with the popular team song, "Meet the Mets" plays its endearing lyrics: "Bring your kiddies. Bring your wife. Guaranteed to have the time of your life!"

No surprise beloved pitcher Tom Seaver, or 'Tom Terrific,' has place of honor here. The three-time Cy Young Award winner is the only team member enshrined in the National Baseball Hall of Fame. We see the very first contract Seaver signed in 1966. The boilerplate vintage document shows the typewritten annual salary amount of $500. Nearby, there's a hat Seaver wore during the winning 1969 season, along with the pitcher's jersey and a signed ball.

However it's the two World Series trophies here that fans flock to the most. The 1969 win spawned the name, 'Miracle Mets,' after their come-from-behind victory. Then in 1986, it was a nail-biting game down to the last minute. The trophies are pride of place – and the ultimate selfie spots – for devoted Mets fans.

**Address** Adjacent to Jackie Robinson Rotunda, Citi Field, 123-01 Roosevelt Avenue, Queens, NY 11368, +1 (718)507-8499, www.mlb.com | **Getting there** Subway to Mets/Willets Point (7); bus to Roosevelt Avenue/Willets Point (Q48), Northern Boulevard/126th Street (Q66) | **Hours** Open during game days | **Tip** The New York Hall of Science offers hands-on experiences with science via interactive exhibits geared for kids (47-01 111th Street, Corona, NY 11368, www.nysci.org).

# 53 __ MMuseumm
*It's okay to look through these peepholes*

If you tire of the big museums, head to Cortlandt Alley in Tribeca to visit a micro museum. Odds are, MMuseumm is like nothing you've seen before. First, the alley itself, with its metal fire escapes, worn brick walls, and colorful graffiti, looks like a scene out of a police drama. In other words, not the kind of place you'd expect to ponder life's complexities. But big ideas are what this little museum does best.

Find your way to number 4, where a pair of black metal, industrial doors are firmly locked shut. Then, like naughty peepholes, two cutouts are set into the doors, allowing you to look inside. It's an abandoned elevator shaft that has been transformed into a curated gallery. Lit 24/7 with an eerie glow, you can peer in at its shallow shelves of collected objects. Call the mobile number posted here, and a recorded message will tell you tidbits about the exhibit.

Started in 2012 by filmmaker Alex Kalman and two colleagues, the idea is to take discarded or everyday objects and consider them in a new way – part art, part journalism. Seemingly insignificant or incongruous objects come together to tell a story about politics, race, war, and humanity. Exhibits change several times a year and touch on ideas like immigration, Isis currency, and handmade objects from Cuba. A second peephole space is right alongside, with an even tinier makeshift gallery. And their Rest Shop sells espresso and trinkets.

If you're lucky, you can visit when the museum is open during part of the week. Only three people at a time fit into the space, and if you are tall, you may have to duck your head. But you'll have the added benefit of a staffer on hand to help visitors understand the theme of the collection. At first, the objects all seem a bit random. Then slowly an idea emerges that casts new meaning on the overlooked or dismissed. Not bad for a museum hidden away in a gritty alley.

**Address** 4 Cortlandt Alley, New York, NY 10013, +1 (888)763-8839, www.mmuseumm.com, info@Mmuseumm.com | **Getting there** Subway to Franklin Street (1, 2), Canal Street (A, C, E, J, N, Q, R, W, Z), City Hall (4, 5, 6) | **Hours** Thu & Fri 6–9pm & Sat & Sun noon–6pm; unrestricted viewing through the peepholes | **Tip** Look for the curious cantilevered balconies of the impressive condo building nearby, designed by Herzog & de Meuron. It's meant to look like a jumble of houses piled up in the sky (56 Leonard Street, New York, NY 10013, www.56leonardtribeca.com).

# 54 MoMA PS 1

*This schoolhouse rocks*

Step into the lobby, and you may hear a little voice saying, "Help me… let your sunshine down." It's coming from over to the left, down in the floorboards, where a tiny video is embedded into a craggy hole. The work of Pipilotti Rist, *Selbstlos im Lavabad* (*Selfless in the Bath of Lava*), shows the Swiss artist standing naked in lava, crying out to visitors above, "I am a worm, and you are a flower." Welcome to MoMA PS 1. And that's just the lobby.

It's the perfect entrée into this former schoolhouse-turned-exhibition-space. Not a collecting institution, their mission is to display the most experimental art in the world. You wander the empty, vintage-tinged hallways; a classroom here, a classroom there. Rotating exhibitions immerse you in videos, paintings, and performances. There's a wonderful sense of discovery here, and you are free to explore.

The iconic *Meeting* (1980–1986) by James Turrell is one work that makes a visit to PS 1 an art pilgrimage. One of the artist's celebrated Skyspaces, it's located on the third floor, where the roof is cut open for a viewing oculus to the sky. Turrell was a key figure in the 1960s California Light and Space Movement. This site-specific work was one of the first Skyspaces he designed, and it inspired him to create many more around the world.

Through a simple door, teak benches line the perimeter, holding some 30 people for an intimate viewing experience. By day, slivers of cloudy or blue sky are visible. There's a faint train whistle in the distance. But at sunset, multi-colored LED lights frame the space, synchronizing with the shifting sun. The effect is hallucinatory. Before your eyes, amber light tones hover like changing auras. Then after 60 minutes or so, the aperture to the sky appears pitch black. It is pure drama, a celestial encounter to remember, by an artist who sculpts with light.

Address 22-25 Jackson Avenue, Long Island City, NY 11101, +1 (718)784-2084, www.momaps1.org, mail_ps1@moma.org | Getting there Subway to Court Square (7), Court Square/23rd Street (E, M) | Hours Mon, Thu – Sun noon – 6pm; see website for Skyspaces viewing times, which change seasonally | Tip For wonderful waterside views of Manhattan, head to Gantry Plaza State Park, a 12-acre oasis that includes manicured gardens and a unique mist fountain (4-09 47th Road, Long Island City, NY 10007, www.parks.ny.gov).

# 55 The Morgan Library & Museum

*Making big deals in a private study*

In its day, the crimson-red study at the Morgan Library was considered among the most beautiful rooms in the world. Maybe it still is. Built by banker and financier John Pierpont Morgan, this environment makes it easy to imagine the passionate collector sitting at the leather-topped desk, puffing his cigar, and a robust fire crackling away. And while most people come here for the towering library, with its astounding collection of texts, this smaller red-walled room is a true delight. It feels like the most personal space, reflecting J.P. Morgan's love of art and beauty.

Built in 1906 by McKim, Meade & White, the library's original concept was not to look forward, but to glance back. Morgan was enamored with the Renaissance, and he indulged that passion with great style. The ruby damask wall coverings bear the Chigi coat of arms, with its mountain and star motifs. The original silk came from an Italian palace, but pollution took its toll, and the present covering was replicated by Scalamandré. It is perfectly sumptuous.

Now look up. The antique wooden ceiling was purchased in Florence and reassembled to fit this room. And all around are stained-glass panels set into the windows, dating from the 15th to 17th centuries. Every detail was tended to, even at the writing desk, where Morgan's initials are artfully tooled into the leather-top design.

This is where Morgan met with art dealers, financiers, and colleagues. Surely this ravishing room cast a spell on all who entered. But the most famous meeting happened here during the 1907 financial crisis, when Morgan literally locked bankers in this suite, while he played solitaire nearby. He forced them to find a solution. They eventually did, pledging their own personal funds to save the banks. No doubt this lavish room captured their hearts – and their wallets.

Address 225 Madison Avenue, New York, NY 10016, +1 (212)685-0008, www.themorgan.org, visitorservices@themorgan.org | Getting there Subway to 33rd Street (6), Grand Central (4, 5, 6, 7), 42nd Street (B, D, F, Q) | Hours Tue–Thu 10:30am–5pm, Fri 10:30am–9pm, Sat 10am–6pm, Sun 11am–6pm | Tip Sip cocktails like a tycoon at the swanky Campbell Bar, in Grand Central Terminal. The restored 1920s space has a glorious Florentine-inspired, hand-painted ceiling (15 Vanderbilt Avenue, New York, NY 10017, www.thecampbellnyc.com).

# 56  Mossman Lock Collection

*A key to the unexpected*

The John M. Mossman Lock Collection is a surprisingly obscure and delightfully quirky discovery. The moment you find it, you'll start worrying that it might one day go away. A museum of locks? Yes, and here's why. It is hosted in an historic building of the General Society of Mechanics and Tradesmen of the City of New York. With its Tiffany front window, marble floors, and soaring curved staircase, this landmark space makes you feel as though you are stepping into a secret club. Go straight ahead for a quick peek into the General Society Library, a hidden city gem. Soaring three stories high, a glorious skylight crowns the reading room, with its polished brass lamps and worn wooden desks. You may very well have this exquisite room to yourself.

The lock museum itself is housed right above you on the second floor. There aren't crowds waiting to get in. More likely, someone will have to escort you up the stairs and turn on the lights. Next, you are handed a vintage book that will be your guide, detailing more than 370 locks, keys, and tools inside the glass cases around the room. You are on your own to explore.

One by one, the specimens, lit with tiny pools of light, are a wonder up close. Nearly every lock here has protected millions in cash or securities, so it's no surprise to see that great attention was paid to their delicate patterns and engravings. Even the insides of the locks, hardly ever seen, are embellished with great care and skill. And like a fine timepiece, some locks have elaborate mechanisms that only open at a certain hour, day, or year. That's precision. Dating from 4000 B.C. onward, this is the personal collection of 19th-century lock maker John Mossman, who was lock-obsessed to be sure. One of the finest assortments in the world, the collection includes many locks that were made for specific vaults. This museum is a unique city treasure, waiting to be unlocked.

Address 20 West 44th Street, New York, NY 10036, +1 (212)840-1840, www.generalsociety.org | Getting there Subway to 42nd Street-Bryant Park (B, D, F, M), 5th Avenue (7), Grand Central (4, 5, 6, 7) | Hours Mon – Fri 11am – 5pm | Tip Across the street is the over-the-top, nautically embellished exterior of the New York Yacht Club, a private club and a Beaux Arts beauty (37 West 44th Street, New York, NY 10036, www.nyyc.org).

# 57 Mount Vernon Hotel

*Day tripping the old-fashioned way*

It's a bit of a miracle that the Mount Vernon Hotel is still standing. Dwarfed and completely enveloped by the steely tall high rises around, this charming 18th-century stone house, right at the foot of the mighty Queensboro Bridge, is easy to miss. But once you spot it, you want to know more.

Actually, this building was never so much a hotel, but more like an 1820s country club, where visitors would gather. Back then, this former carriage house was solidly in the country, set on a bluff overlooking the East River and its parade of boats passing by. It was the perfect getaway from the summer stench of lower Manhattan, where garbage-eating pigs were running free in the streets.

Once inside the lively Tavern Room, you can easily imagine the male guests talking and toasting. There are beer kegs and a bar, where spirits were served. Those dog-bowl looking green receptacles all around are actually spittoons because the art of tobacco chewing was taken seriously. Newspapers were read, politics debated, all while playing cribbage at the game tables set up in the space. It was a sort of 19th-century man cave.

It's a different story upstairs, where the ladies lounged in this finely appointed parlor devoted to music. A tall harp takes center stage, conjuring up the sweet sound from its strings. Flutes and pianos would also be played, in harmony with birds singing in cages for a masterful mix. Then, at around 2pm, the men and women would gather together in the dining room for a special meal. Set today with cheery blue-and-white transferware, the elegant offerings conjure up images of turtle stew being served, which was all the rage. So too were oysters and fruit pies. Finally, make your way to the secret garden in the back, where flowers and herbs flourish even today. This old hotel, concealed in this high rise canyon of Manhattan, is a lovely time capsule of leisurely life.

Address 421 East 61st Street, New York, NY 10065, +1 (212)838-6878, www.mvhm.org, info@mvhm.org | Getting there Subway to Lexington Avenue-59th Street (N, R, 4, 5, 6), Lexington Avenue-63rd Street (F) | Hours Tue–Sun 11am–4pm | Tip Take a bit of a carnival ride, right in the city, on the Roosevelt Island Tramway. You are suspended above the East River, as your glassed-in tram glides over to Roosevelt Island, all for the cost of a subway ride (East 59th Street & 2nd Avenue, New York, NY 10022, www.rioc.gov).

# 58_Museum of the American Gangster

*An offer you can't refuse*

You'll discover booze, bullets, and bedlam in the two-room Museum of the American Gangster, located above a former speakeasy on a sleepy East Village street. The intertwined tales of prohibition and organized crime are fleshed out within the confines of a once-rollicking brothel. In the back room, you'll see an unwieldy, Appalachian copper still used to make moonshine. It sits alongside a Tommy automated weapon and a doctor's prescription for alcohol. All these displays are potent symbols of Prohibition and how organized crime flourished because of it.

The colorful, enthusiastic, guided tour makes these two simple rooms come alive. You'll find the bullet that killed gangster Pretty Boy Floyd, along with the shell casing from the Bonnie and Clyde car in which Clyde Barrow was killed. Two plaster, ivory-colored death masks of John Dillinger, the bank robber who was killed by FBI agents in 1934, sit side by side in a glass case. The visages look menacing even at rest.

Opened in 2010, the museum is an ode to crime for founder Lorcan Otway, who grew up in the building. His father bought 78 and 80 Saint Marks Place in 1964 to open a theater. The younger Otway inherited it and became fascinated with the tales of what went on inside. Those stories come alive when you don a hard hat and make your way to the former 1920s speakeasy below. Now a theater, flappers and bootleggers once danced to the sounds of jazz bands. Chicago gangster Al Capone was said to visit here along with politicians and police officials. You can almost hear the revelry.

In the cellar below, you'll see where the speakeasy's shadowy owner, Frank Hoffman, played cards and counted cash, along with a safe that was opened in the 1960s. It contained two million dollars in gold certificates, all expired, in true gangster style.

**Address** 80 Saint Marks Place, New York, NY 10003, +1 (212)228-5736, www.museumoftheamericangangster.org | **Getting there** Subway to 1st Avenue (L), Astor Place (6), 2nd Avenue (F) | **Hours** Daily 1–6pm | **Tip** Visit a modern-day speakeasy at Please Don't Tell. Enter through a phone booth inside Crif Dogs (113 Saint Marks Place, New York, NY 10009, www.pdtnyc.com).

# 59 Museum of Arts and Design

*Elevating handmade heritage*

Right in the shadow of the looming Time Warner Center, stands this lively museum where there's always an atmosphere of discovery. From sculpture to furniture, jewelry to ceramics, this bright contemporary space is all about the idea of making things.

Drop by one of the open Artist Studios, where you can see artists and designers at work. It could be a ceramic artist, a jewelry maker, or a textile designer. You can meet the artists, watch them work, and ask them questions or discuss ideas. It's much like visiting an artist friend in their private studio.

Elsewhere in the museum, four floors offer rotating exhibitions with a fresh perspective on people, process, and materials. You may see a collection of lapel pins by former Secretary of State Madeleine Albright; the digitally designed furniture by American master Wendell Castle; or the embroidery and tie-dyes of 1960s flower children. The topics are original and enlightening. Make sure to visit the Tiffany & Co. Foundation Jewelry Gallery, which is the only space in the country devoted exclusively to modern and contemporary art jewelry. Sparkling glass cases hold covetable pieces from the museum's permanent collection. Then check out the secret Study Storage Collection against the wall, where you can pull out stacks of drawers filled with jeweled treasures.

Before you leave, stop by the gift shop, which is the chic New Yorker's best-kept secret. Here you'll find unique jewelry and artist-made objects like bronze cuffs, gilded papier-mâché bowls, and gravity-defying champagne flutes. Then for a treat, take the elevator to the museum's top-floor restaurant, Robert. With its floor-to-ceiling wall of windows you will be hovering over Central Park and Columbus Circle with some of the best views in the city.

**Address** 2 Columbus Circle, New York, NY 10019, +1 (212)299-7777, www.madmuseum.org, info@madmuseum.org | **Getting there** Subway to Columbus Circle/59th Street (A, B, C, D, 1, 2), 57th Street/7th Avenue (N, Q, R, W) | **Hours** Tue & Wed, Fri–Sun 10am–6pm, Thu 10am–9pm | **Tip** Take in an exhibition at the venerable and beautiful Art Students League nearby, where artists like Helen Frankenthaler, Georgia O'Keefe, Jackson Pollack, Cy Twombly, and Ai Wei Wei have studied (215 West 57th Street, New York, NY 10019, www.theartstudentsleague.org).

# 60 Museum of Chinese in America

*Coming to America*

With bustling streets, blinking neon signs, and beguiling shops, New York's Chinatown is a lively adventure and a great place for a stroll. Dig under the surface of the community at the Museum of Chinese in America, with a curated message. Street sounds fade as you pass through the towering glass door into the quiet, where brick walls and soaring windows embrace.

Designed by architect Maya Lin, the minimal lines evoke rooms inside a simple, family home. Meander through to experience the complicated and compelling story of Chinese Americans.

In an innovative, immersive installation, you'll find stirring sights and sounds within these darkly lit galleries, which tell the early immigrants' tales. From speakers imbedded into the walls, you hear 19th-century diary entries read aloud, short snippets of daily life and the intense desire to belong. Chinese immigrants were not allowed to work in the skilled trades, so they found employment in the service industries: cooking, child care, and housekeeping. The most arduous choice, the Eight Pound Livelihood, is a reference to the weight of an iron and the ubiquitous laundry industry in which these workers toiled. One such iron is here for you to pick up. The sheer weight of the small implement is surprising and helps you literally feel the plight of these immigrants, who wielded irons just like this one for long hours.

Nearby, menus from popular chop suey restaurants show an Americanized cuisine that was both exotic and familiar. Movie posters display Hollywood images of Chinese-Americans in the entertainment industry. And the recreation of a general store stocks herbs, teas, textiles, and ceramics; immersing you in early commerce. Finally, illuminated panels pay homage to contemporary Chinese-Americans, like fashion designer Vera Wang and cellist Yo-Yo Ma.

**Address** 215 Centre Street, New York, NY 10013, +1 (855)955-6622, www.mocanyc.org, info@mocanyc.org | **Getting there** Subway to Canal Street (6, J, N, Q, R, W, Z) | **Hours** Tue & Wed, Fri–Sun 11am–6pm, Thu 11am–9pm | **Tip** Stop by the Mahayana Buddhist Temple, where you'll see what may be the largest Buddha in the city. This 16-foot-tall gold statue is adorned with a dramatic blue halo (133 Canal Street, New York, NY 10002, www.en.mahayana.us).

# 61 Museum of the City of New York

*Curating the Big Apple*

In a city filled with museums, it takes some chutzpah to call yourself the Museum of the City of New York. But chutzpah is what it's got, and a visit to this Upper East Side institution only deepens the joys of being a New Yorker. At its heart is the dynamic New York at It's Core exhibition that shows how New York City became the Big Apple. In chic, darkly lit rooms, we see key objects that tell the tale of money, diversity, density, and creativity. It's a remarkable journey.

Take the iconic Statue of Liberty. The museum has the early maquettes that French sculptor Frédéric Auguste Bartholdi used for the 1886 design. You can see how Bartholdi tried to get the arm, draping, and tilt of the body just right. Nearby, a handsome pair of 1900s kid-leather, lace-up boots capture the city's rise as a center of commerce when palaces of shopping, or department stores, turned buying into a leisure sport.

In the 1920s, the Jazz Age comes alive. By now, one third of the population was born abroad. African-Americans left the south after World War I and made Harlem the nation's go-to Black urban community. We see rare, vintage jazz albums, tap shoes, and a sassy red velvet flapper dress, all delights of the Roaring Twenties.

In the post-World War ll exhibit, a well-used metal paint can from artist Jackson Pollock is thrilling to see up close. Known for his breakthrough 'action paintings,' he would drip paint onto canvases. Even the paint can itself is filled with drips (see ch. 67). The 1970s get their due with the iconic disco Studio 54. A hand-scribbled guest list from a single Friday night in 1978 boasts an inspiring mix of celebrities like Peter Frampton, Ringo Starr, and Liberace. Be sure not to miss the Future City Lab, which looks to the new challenges ahead, proving New York's fast moving, ever forward motion.

Address 1220 5th Avenue, New York, NY 10029, +1 (212)534-1672, www.mcny.org, info@mcny.org | Getting there Subway to 103rd Street (6), 110th Street (2, 3) | Hours Daily 10am–6pm | Tip Across the street, take a stroll through the extraordinary, six-acre formal plantings of The Conservatory Garden in Central Park ((5th Avenue at 105th Street, www.centralparknyc.org/things-to-see-and-do/attractions/conservatory-garden).

# 62 — Museum at Eldridge Street

*Awe-inspiring interior*

When preservationists first encountered the Eldridge Street Synagogue in the 1990s, pigeons were roosting inside. Dust on the benches was so thick, you could write your initials. Twenty years and some 20 million dollars later, this architectural jewel box is one of the most astonishing spaces in New York City. And the little museum they created here is one of the city's best. No small feat.

The location itself is a surprise. Here amidst the makeshift dumpling and noodle shops of Chinatown, you see the soaring 1887 edifice with its rich stained-glass windows and graceful Moorish lines. Built by Eastern European Jews, this was an immigrant's exuberant declaration of worship. But as the congregation dwindled, the building fell into disrepair. If not for a dedicated group of architects and artists, it would be lost.

Their restoration work is joyous to behold. Follow one of their intimate tours, and you are connected to the space and all its details, large and small, like the massive brass, central chandelier that reigns over the sanctuary. All 400 pieces were taken apart, refurbished, and rewired. It now casts an atmospheric, amber glow through stained-glass windows all around. On the walls, original hand-painted stenciling has been brought back. The charming irregularity of the designs is poignant proof of the human hand at work – not machine made. See if you can find a heart motif embedded into the folk-like style.

Then for a final flourish, the monumental, blue-starred circular window designed by contemporary artist Kiki Smith and architect Deborah Gans is set over the historic sanctuary. The original was damaged by weather in the 1940s. This resplendent replacement, installed in 2010, positively glows. It is the museum's centerpiece. It marks the continuing evolution of this hidden treasure, a perfect aesthetic blending of old and new.

Address 12 Eldridge Street, New York, NY 10002, +1 (212)219-0302, www.eldridgestreet.org, info@eldridgestreet.org | Getting there Subway to East Broadway (F), Grand Street (B, D), Canal Street (6, J, N, Q, R, W, Z) | Hours Sun–Thu 10am–5pm, Fri 10am–3pm; check website for tour times | Tip Taste a real New York bagel, along with every spread imaginable, at the historic Kossar's Bakery (367 Grand Street, New York, NY 10002, www.kossars.com).

# 63__The Museum at FIT

*New York's most stylish museum*

From coats to capes, and ball gowns to outerwear, the culture of fashion is the mission at this beloved museum filled with sartorial surprises. Housed inside the Fashion Institute of Technology (FIT), this is where you can revel in fashions from the past, while glimpsing clothing concepts for the future.

The main floor Fashion & Textile History Gallery is a feast of dresses, gowns, hats, and trousers. Drawing on a permanent collection of 50,000 pieces, there is a staggering assortment to choose from. Selections rotate every six months but always cover 250 years of fashion history. Look for designers like Balenciaga, Dior, Chanel, Halston, and Yves Saint Laurent. Shoe-obsessed fans, step right up and prepare yourself for shoe envy: the museum archive holds 4,000 pairs. You'll also see hats, lingerie, swimwear, and costume jewelry. Viewed up close, it's the small details that delight, including delicate pleats, graceful collars, and bold prints. Immersed inside these quiet galleries, it's easy to understand the intersection between fashion and art.

Part of the fun here is watching the FIT design students milling about. With sketch pads in hand, groups of them peer closely at a garment and carefully examine the pockets, cuffs, and hem. It's a treat to see what they are wearing and to guess who might be the design star of the future.

On the lower level, temporary exhibitions offer fresh perspectives and sometimes push stylistic boundaries. It might be a look at corsets, contemporary ideas on denim, or gothic inspired dark glamor. The emphasis is on 'directional' looks that shape fashion history, featuring current designers like Vivienne Westwood, Rick Owens, or Rei Kawakubo. Try to plan your visit to the museum in May, when FIT design students are showing their graduation projects. It's a real life *Project Runway*, and you get to be the judge.

Address 227 West 27th Street, New York, NY 10001, +1 (212)217-4558, www.fitnyc.edu, museuminfo@fitnyc.edu | Getting there Subway to 28th Street (1, N, R), 23rd Street (A, C, E, F) | Hours Tue–Fri noon–8pm, Sat 10am–5pm | Tip Take in one of the interactive performances at the McKittrick Hotel, a lively warehouse, turned into experiential theater that is highly original and quirky (530 West 27th Street, New York, NY 10001).

# 64 Museum of Food and Drink

*The science of savory and sweet*

The first thing that hits you is the aroma. On this day, it's freshly baked fortune cookies with just a hint of orange. The scent is a prelude of what's in store at the Museum of Food and Drink (MOFAD), a Brooklyn temple to food and drink.

Located in a former garage with a modern warehouse vibe, this place is part hipster lab, part coffee shop. Head over to one of the Smell Machines, and anything you thought you knew about food might be challenged. The Coffee Smell Machine reveals how some of our most beloved aromas hide a secret. Push one button, and the faint smell of stale coffee wafts out of a metal tube. Push another button, and a skunky, sulfur-smelling chemical hits you. Push both buttons, and the heavenly scent of coffee is perfect, showing us even a tiny amount of a flavor, unpleasant on its own, can make another dull flavor pop. The even more elaborate Smell Synth Machine combines dozens of flavors to dizzying effects with smells like grass, orange peel, lavender, and overripe fruit.

The brainchild of former sculptor Dave Arnold, the museum found funding with a Kickstarter campaign in 2013. Rotating special exhibitions chronicle the journey of food, like the history of Chinese-American restaurants and cuisine. They also offer occasional cooking classes, guided tastings, and hands-on workshops.

And if all this talk of food is making you hungry, a special Culinary Studio allows you to sit a spell and interact with a rotating roster of chefs. Before your eyes, they will create dishes like Jasmine Rice Pudding, explaining techniques such as stir fry, wok, and velveting. Any questions you have about cooking and cuisine, they will attempt to answer. With true Brooklyn chutzpah, the museum's aim is to become the world's authority on food and drink, one day, one exhibition at a time.

Address 62 Bayard Street, Brooklyn, NY 11222, +1 (718)387-2845, www.mofad.org, info@mofad.org | Getting there Subway to Lorimer or Bedford (L), Nassau or Metropolitan (G) | Hours Fri–Sun noon–6pm | Tip For the ultimate hand-crafted cocktail, walk to the Shanty, a sleek bar set right inside the New York Distilling Company, a gin distillery that also offers tours with tastings (79 Richardson Street, Brooklyn, NY 11222, www.nydistilling.com).

# 65 Museum of Jewish Heritage

*A living memorial to the Holocaust*

Located across the Hudson River from Ellis Island and the Statue of Liberty, the museum's granite building makes the first impression – a six-sided shape reminiscent of the six-pointed Star of David. It's the perfect framework to highlight the rich tapestry of Jewish life before, during, and after the Holocaust. It is New York's uniquely global responsibility never to forget.

With three floors of exhibition space, there is much to see. Start with the museum's core exhibition, which consists of two floors filled with some 800 objects and 2,000 photos, a visual and auditory journey through Jewish history. Beginning in the 1880s, simple artifacts become touchstones, like a wedding canopy, or huppah, along with a 1924 lace wedding dress, and a men's wedding tunic or *kittel*. There are Torahs and sacred artifacts from synagogues.

Then one floor up, the mood shifts. The galleries here are devoted to the War Against the Jews, where objects, images, and voices tell the Holocaust story. The rise of Nazism and anti-Semitism is told with original film showing impactful survival testimony. These voices punctuate the artifacts all around, and personalize history in a most moving way. Still, there are objects of optimism folded in, like a well-worn trumpet on display that musician Louis Bannet played in the Auschwitz-Birkenau inmate orchestra. A final section shows renewal after World War II, when Jewish families sought to rebuild their lives and bring Nazis to justice.

Afterwards, visit the outdoor Garden of Stones, the perfect place for reflection, created by artist Andy Goldsworthy in 2003. In this permanent installation, 18 boulders were hollowed out, and a single sapling was planted in each one by a Holocaust survivor. The trees have grown, fusing with the stone to become stronger.

Postcard from the Kutno Ghetto
From M. Eisner to Roman Eisner in the Bronx, in Polish.
Kutno Ghetto, Poland, January 7, 1942.
Gift of Roman Eisner, Yaffa Eliach Collection donated by
the Center for Holocaust Studies

"I still don't understand why I have only
received two letters from you...I beg you
with bitter tears to save me."

Roman Eisner

Postcard from the Lodz Ghetto
From Eduard and Paula Frisch to Heinrich and
Zdenka Frisch in Prague, in German. Lodz Ghetto, Poland,
June 15, 1941.
Gift of Mehnt and Paul Köllet

"We are very concerned that our many cards
leave us without any news from you...If you
knew of our longing you would rush to reply."

Eduard and Paula Frisch

Postcard from the Warsaw Ghetto
From Lodzia Gase Kavraner to Solomon Gass in
New York City, in Polish. Warsaw Ghetto, Poland,
October 9, 1941.
Gift of Fred Rosenthal

"Concerning our economic situation, we
cannot say anything positive. Our health is
not good...My little son has become sick."

Lodzia Gase Kavraner

Postcard from Modliborzyce Ghetto
From Ella Riegler to Max Birnbach in Switzerland, in
German. Modliborzyce Ghetto, Poland, August 13, 1942.
Gift of Max Birnbach

"I ask you please, do everything possible, think
constantly about me, and don't forget me."
Riegler, a friend of Birnbach's aunt in the
Ghetto, was writing on her behalf.

Max Birnbach

Postcard from the Terezin Ghetto
From Paul Mahrer to Betty Mahrer in Leitmeritz, in German.
Terezin Ghetto, Czechoslovakia, October 10, 1943.
Gift of Jerome and Carolyn Mahrer

There was a limit on the number of postcards
Ghetto inmates were allowed to send. Paul
Mahrer signed the postcard with the name of a
relative in order to mail yet another to his wife.

Paul Mahrer

Postcard from the Wolbrom Ghetto
From Regina Grossfeld to Bela Borenstein in Brownsville.
Soderststraat, in German. Wolbrom Ghetto, Poland, October
8, 1941. Gift of Bella Reinert, Yaffa Eliach Collection
donated by the Center for Holocaust Studies

"You can't imagine how pleased I am that I can
write a few words to you. May God help all of
us be together in happiness."

Background photo: Trying to maintain contact
with the outside world, a Warsaw Ghetto

Address 36 Battery Place, New York, NY 10280, +1 (646)437-4202, www.mjhnyc.org,
info@mjhnyc.org | Getting there Subway to Bowling Green (4, 5), Rector Street (1),
Whitehall or Rector Street (R) | Hours Sun–Tue 10am–6pm, Wed & Thu 10am–8pm,
Fri 10am–5pm | Tip Walk along the Battery Park City Esplanade, a riverfront park that
has postcard-perfect views of the Statue of Liberty and beyond (runs entire length of
Battery Park City from Stuyvesant High School to Battery Park, www.bpcparks.org).

# 66 Museum of Mathematics
*A cool equation*

Open the cheeky front door, with the π (pi)-shaped handle, and you know this is someplace special: a quirky, tricked-out playground dedicated to math. Yes, math. Never mind those terrifying school exams calculating logarithms. Here, you explore the beauty and wonder of mathematics, one activity at a time. Laid out across two floors, interactive games appeal to a sense of play, unlocking knowledge at every turn.

A big disco floor comes to mind when hopping on the interactive Math Square. Step on and move around. The electronic floor is programmed to light up paths from one person to the next. Even the slightest movement changes the colorful paths with lightning speed.

Ever see a tricycle with square wheels? You can ride one around in circles and learn how a specially designed track uses an exact, three-dimensional surface to guide the bike along, keeping the axle level as the wheel rotates. Seems you *can* reinvent the wheel. And you can reinvent the tree too. The Human Tree demonstrates the idea of fractal images for both young and old. Stand, arms out, in front of the special screen, and your silhouette repeats itself into branches and leaves before your eyes – tiny images of yourself over and over. Strangely beautiful.

A first in the US, this brainy carnival uses some 30 aesthetically designed mini exhibitions to encourage discovery. All those friendly workers with the yellow shirts are here to guide you along, immersing you in this interactive wonderland.

And if you find yourself in need of a break, take a seat at the Enigma Café. They don't serve food here, but instead, brain teasing, sculptural wooden puzzles. Fitting the pieces together is frustrating and fun. And just listening to those around you tackling the same task is amusing. But be forewarned, the Six Cushion Shot and the Patience Puzzles can be especially challenging.

**Address** 11 East 26th Street, New York, NY 10010, +1 (212)542-0566, www.momath.org, info@momath.org | **Getting there** Subway to 23rd Street (6, F, M, N, R, W) | **Hours** Daily 10am–5pm | **Tip** Across the street, Madison Square Park is actually an arboretum, or a tree museum. You can even take summer garden walking tours of their lush plantings (www.madisonsquarepark.org).

# 67 Museum of Modern Art

*Deliberate drips*

Brimming with heart-stopping works by titans of the art world – Picasso, Matisse, Van Gogh – MoMA is a museum where you may not know where to begin. So find your way to the calm corner where one painting stands especially tall. *One: Number 31, 1950* by Jackson Pollock (1912–1956) dwarfs mere humans with its immense size. Nearly 9 feet high and 17 feet wide, the massive canvas fills an entire wall. It's not a painting of a person or thing, but a complex surface filled with pulsing threads of paint. They arc and dance, exploding off the canvas. It is pure energy.

A masterpiece of abstract expressionism, the work astounds us even today. Pollock pushed painting into a new dimension by taking the canvas off the easel and onto the floor. He then flung and dripped paint all over the surface in a rhythmic dance, allowing chance and gravity to play along. "On the floor, I am more at ease," Pollock said. "I feel nearer, more a part of the painting, since this way I can walk around it, work from the four sides and literally be *in* the painting."

At first the work feels random. Then an order takes shape: skeins of gray, blue, and beige, interlaced with black and white loops. You imagine the artist's arm sweeping across the canvas with great power and speed. The paint is both shiny and matte. Thick, then thin. Hypnotic and mesmerizing. It's a record of a painting being made, right down to an actual fly imbedded into the pigment on the lower right side. See if you can spot it.

Only when Pollock stepped back did he glimpse what the work was about. It is a snapshot of his inner self, a psychological self-portrait, influenced by World War II and the postwar period. This work made abstract expression the first uniquely American art movement and also made New York the center of the art world. An iconic work in an iconic museum, this painting embodies that time on a grand scale.

Address 11 West 53rd Street, New York, NY 10019, +1 (212)708-9400, www.moma.org, info@moma.org | Getting there Fifth Avenue/53rd Street (E, M), 7th Avenue (B, D), 57th Street/7th Avenue (N, Q, R, W) | Hours Sat–Thu 10:30am–5:30pm, Fri 10:30am–8pm | Tip Enjoy a relaxing drink across the street in the dazzling, crystal-filled lounge at the Baccarat Hotel (28 West 53rd Street, New York, NY 10019, www.baccarathotels.com).

# 68 Museum of the Moving Image

*Oscar The Grouch would approve*

It turns out that the best way to get to Sesame Street may be via the Museum of the Moving Image in Queens. An immersive, colorful exhibition installed on the second floor of the museum is a fun romp through the muppet-filled world of puppet master Jim Henson. You may never want to leave.

The mission of this museum is to advance understanding, enjoyment, and appreciation of film, television, and digital media. One of the most beloved exhibits focuses on the magic of the Muppets. Wind your way through a series of small galleries that are designed to dazzle the kids and artfully amuse the adults. Videos of Jim Henson highlight the brilliance of the genius puppeteer, who died from an infection in 1990 at the age of 53. You can get up close with the fuzzy green Kermit, whose simple face seems alive. It's an expressiveness that is created through the relative placement of the eyes, nose, and mouth, what Henson's team called "the magic triangle." You can also try your hand at designing your own Muppet. Pick out a wig and add Velcro-backed magic triangle features. It's a completely engrossing experience.

You'll see Miss Piggy looking resplendent in a wedding dress. The iconic puppet was first designed and built in 1974 by Henson company member Bonnie Erickson, who initially named her Miss Piggy Lee after singer Peggy Lee. Prairie Dawn is here wearing her floral prairie dress alongside the saxophone-playing Zoot puppet, a hipster for sure.

Finally, don't miss the life-sized, yellow-feathered Big Bird, who was the most difficult puppet to perform. You learn how the puppeteer had to extend his right arm above his head to operate the mouth and eyes while watching a small body monitor strapped to a harness. The museum also offers movie screenings ranging from Muppet movies, to classic films, to campy favorites, often accompanied by panel discussions.

Address 36-01 35th Avenue, Queens, NY 11106, +1 (718)777-6800, www.movingimage.us, info@movingimage.org | Getting there Subway to Steinway Street (M, R), Broadway (N, W), 40th Street (7) | Hours Wed & Thu 10:30am–5pm, Fri 10:30am–8pm, Sat & Sun 10:30am–6pm | Tip Visit the waterside Socrates Sculpture Park, with its outdoor, large-scale sculptures. The lovely site was actually once an abandoned landfill (32-01 Vernon Boulevard, Long Island City, NY 11106, www.socratessculpturepark.org).

# 69 Museum of Reclaimed Urban Space

*They're taking over!*

Think of this very small, grass-roots museum as a 'power to the people' kind of place. No long lines or trendy architecture – just a make-shift storefront and the desire to tell a story of social activism.

The museum building itself says a lot. Housed inside the infamous C-Squat, this was the epicenter for a movement starting in the 1970s to reclaim abandoned buildings. Musicians squatted in, or took over, this very building, and they've been living in apartments above ever since. Step inside the lobby, and you are visually immersed in this neighborhood movement. You'll see walls of graffiti, protest pamphlets, even barricade signs, *Police Line; Do Not Cross*. Beneath your feet, there's a carpet of colorful protest stencils spray-painted right onto the floorboards. A counterculture collage.

"People did an amazing thing here," museum director Bill DiPaola explains. "They reclaimed city space in a community way, not a corporate way." Head downstairs to the tiny, 19th-century, brick-walled basement, and you're in protest headquarters. A video shows neighborhood demonstrations, along with local efforts to establish bike lanes in the city. On the wall, a purple tie-dye tunic pays tribute to a beloved activist, while a bicycle-powered generator hails from Occupy Wall Street movements.

But it's in the many community gardens nearby where you'll see urban activism in full bloom. Dotting the neighborhood, these former empty lots were turned into green spaces in the 1970s. And in this densely populated neighborhood, they have remained a vital part of daily life. "This is where we grew food to survive," DiPaola recalls. "And all the recycling efforts you see in the city today – they were started right here." That's the very reason the tiny museum and gardens have survived; to pass the people's revolution on to the next generation.

Address 155 Avenue C, New York, NY 10009, +1 (646)340-8341, www.morusnyc.org, info@morusnyc.org | Getting there Subway to 1st Avenue (L), 2nd Avenue (F) | Hours Tue, Thu–Sun 11am–7pm | Tip Visit one of the most iconic community gardens, La Plaza Cultural, with its artful green space and performance area (East 9th Street & Avenue C, New York, NY 10003, www.opencity.com/laplazacultural).

# 70__Museum of Sex
*I'm not blushing – you're blushing*

On any given day, you'll find a continuous party going on at the seductively popular Museum of Sex, a daring idea that draws visitors in droves. Located right across the street from the bustling Madison Square Park, the museum offers an experience like no other. Since the museum first opened in 2002, its mission has been to preserve and present the history of human sexuality and the ways it has evolved and affected society. It's high-minded, but your mind is also welcome to go elsewhere.

You'll walk through the brightly lit gift shop first, where candy-colored sex toys are arranged all around. There are kitschy cards, scant costumes, feather masks, and passion flower herbs. Business is brisk amidst a lively atmosphere of play, proof that S-E-X does indeed sell. Next, purchase your tickets and make your way into the dimly lit exhibition galleries. Quickly the mood darkens, as specially designed blacked-out windows add a sense of secrecy and surprise.

But exhibitions here do try to both titillate and inform. The Sex Life of Animals presents the birds and bees like never before, with life-sized sculptures of pandas and deer mating as if nobody's watching. The history of sexuality in the city is explored with an 1855 New York brothel guide, erotic turn-of-the-century photographs, and a 19th-century, hand-illustrated sex manual. Other popular exhibits show explicit imagery from the Greeks to the 1972 film *Deep Throat*. With a museum collection of more than 20,000 objects, you'll see art, photography, clothing, historic ephemera, films, and videos. The museum has a seemingly endless erotic archive.

Especially popular is the sultry bar on the ground floor, where enticing cocktails range from demure to kinky. Don't miss the fun house-inspired Jump for Joy Bouncy Castle of Breasts, a room filled with giant inflatable boobs, where you can indeed jump for joy.

Address 233 5th Avenue, New York, NY 10016, +1 (212)689-6337, www.museumofsex.com, info@museumofsex.com | Getting there Subway to 28th Street/Broadway (R), 28th Street/Park Avenue (6), 28th Street/7th Avenue (1) | Hours Sun – Thu 10:30am – 10pm, Fri & Sat 10:30am – 11pm | Tip Try your photo skills nearby in front of the triangular, iconic Flatiron Building, a beloved landmark – and a popular selfie spot (175 5th Avenue, New York, NY 10010).

# 71 National Arts Club

*For the love of arts*

Of all the private, old-world clubs in Manhattan, the National Arts Club is one that you must experience. It's located across the street from Gramercy Park, the glorious, gated park accessible only to privileged nearby residents lucky enough to have a key. That air of exclusivity extends to this 1840s Victorian Gothic Revival masterpiece. Most people don't realize that their regular art exhibitions are open to the public. A quick visit here is like being a club member for an hour without the hefty dues.

Step through the front door and see the grandeur of the place with its inlaid floors, dark paneled walls, and shimmering chandeliers. As you make your way to the first-floor gallery, you'll pass a hallway filled with the glorious portraits of demure Gilded Age beauties. And anchoring it all is an enormous wooden newel post lamp in the shape of a goddess. You get the idea she has seen a lot of drama standing here all these years.

The club was established in 1898 to gather artists of all genres as well as art lovers and patrons. The mission remains the same today, and they rotate a variety of exhibitions in their four galleries. It might be a series of photographs celebrating the beauty and grace of black women by Kamoinge Inc., a pioneering collective of African and African-American photographers. Or it could be selections from the club's archives, including tidbits from famous past members such as a letter from actress Lillian Hellman asking club board members to stop their gossip. The history here is deep and rich. It is worthwhile to keep your eye on the exhibits schedule to make sure you get to see them all.

Try to peek at the little portrait gallery on the first-floor landing. Every inch of the wall space is hung with an amazing collection of sketches and photographs including dozens of past recipients of club awards. Standing inside this sanctuary of civility in Gramercy Park, you can sense its great history.

**Address** 15 Gramercy Park South, New York, NY 10003, +1 (212)475-3424, www.nationalartsclub.org | **Getting there** Subway to 23rd Street (6), 14th Street/ Union Square (4, 5, N, Q, R, W) | **Hours** Mon–Fri 10am–5pm (check website for specific exhibition times, which can vary) | **Tip** Don't miss the glorious ironwork of The Players, an iconic private club in a Gothic Revival building next door (16 Gramercy Park South, New York, NY 10003, www.theplayersnyc.org).

# 72 National Jazz Museum in Harlem

*Take the 'A' train*

What this petite museum in the heart of Harlem lacks in size it more than makes up for in swing. You are immersed in jazz history from the past bracketed by the music scene of today. Front and center is the museum's highlight, Duke Ellington's baby grand piano. Painted a warm white, the piano was purchased by the rising bandleader in the 1920s during the heyday of the Cotton Club. Ellington went on to compose iconic works on these keys, including, "It Don't Mean a Thing if it Ain't Got That Swing" and "Sophisticated Lady." The piano sits near a recreated 1940s Harlem living room, the frequent gathering place to socialize and hear music.

You'll also see a saxophone played by Eddie 'Lockjaw' Davis, who earned his nickname because of the firm lock his jaws had on the mouthpiece. Through an interactive touchscreen exhibit, you can explore his recordings, family scrapbooks, and personal artifacts. Nearby you'll see cases filled with jazz-related ephemera, like a poster for a Sunday afternoon bebop concert with Dinah Washington. There are early art deco-styled jazz catalogs from Columbia Records. Through "Harlem Rent Party" invitations, friends and neighbors offered music in their apartments or brownstones to help someone pay rent. For a dose of style, there is the double-breasted wool coat worn by Benny Carter on the night his band reopened the Apollo Theater in 1934 and established the venue as a Harlem hotspot.

But what would a jazz museum be without music? At the National Jazz Museum, you are invited to pull up a chair and listen to a rare sound archive on a pair of headphones. Meticulously recorded by Bill Savory in the 1930s, the entire collection was undiscovered until 2010. It contains private rehearsals and sessions by Ellington, Goodman, and Holiday recorded in the nearby buildings and streets.

Address 58 West 129th Street, New York, NY 10027, +1 (212)348-8300, www.jazzmuseuminharlem.org | Getting there Subway to 125th Street (A, B, C, D, 2, 3, 4, 5, 6)| Hours Thu–Mon 11am–5pm | Tip Have a bite at the Red Rooster, chef Marcus Samuelsson's Ethiopian/Southern/Swedish bistro, particularly its stellar Sunday Gospel Brunch (310 Lenox Avenue, New York, NY 10027, www.redroosterharlem.com).

# 73__National Museum of the American Indian

*The beauty of Native life*

The New York branch of the Smithsonian's National Museum of the American Indian is housed in the Alexander Hamilton US Customs House, one of the most sumptuous Beaux Arts buildings in the city. It's the perfect place to explore this museum and its impressive collections. The permanent exhibition, Infinity of Nations, is a must see and contains over 700 works that immerses visitors in Native cultures.

Start your visit with the dazzling display of Native headdresses and experience sheer artistry and the undeniable link between humans and the natural world. A Yoeme deer dance headdress features a small deer head atop an ivory colored cap. The headdress symbolizes the tribe's bond with the animal world. An elaborate red feathered headdress or cape might be worn for a child's naming ceremony or boy's initiation.

There are collections of baskets, moccasins, and ceramics throughout the museum that are artfully embellished and perfectly useful. An 1850s buffalo hide, also known as a Warrior's Exploit Robe, and one of the few remaining in existence, depicts important military exploits with simple line drawings. An especially poignant artifact is the Inuit Woman's Inner Parka, which is constructed of caribou skin and trimmed with some 160,000 beads. Its broad shoulders enabled a mother to slip her baby from her back to the front for nursing and served as a necessary garment during the cold Hudson Bay winters.

At the same time, there are many more recent current artifacts. One of the most fascinating is a 2002 Jingle Dress, with jingles fashioned out of lined notebook paper, making a rustling sound when the dress is worn. Artist Maria Hupfield says it's an homage to indigenous writers, whose names are inscribed in each jingle.

Address 1 Bowling Green, New York, NY 10004, +1 (212)514-3700, www.nmai.si.edu |
Getting there Subway to Bowling Green (4, 5), Rector Street or South Ferry (1), Whitehall
Street (R), Broad Street (J, Z), Wall Street (2, 3) | Hours Daily 10am–5pm, Thu until 8pm |
Tip One block north of the museum stands *Charging Bull*, a bronze sculpture installed by
Arturo Di Modica originally as guerilla art and now an iconic Financial District symbol
(Broadway & Morris, New York, NY 10004, www.chargingbull.com).

# 74 National September 11 Memorial & Museum

*A powerful remembrance*

It is no easy task to design a museum chronicling the 9/11 terrorist attacks. And it was daunting to build the National September 11 Memorial Museum in such close proximity to where the Twin Towers stood. Twisted metal beams, a burned fire truck, news clips, missing-person signs, candles, clocks, and children's drawings are parts of the emotional array of artifacts and sounds that bring you into the trauma of that day. There is a lot to absorb and understand. You should plan on spending three or four hours going through all of the exhibits.

The massive wall in the Memorial Hall is a spiritual resting spot for visitors. Composed of vivid blue squares, it's a work of art that causes you to stop and reflect. The work by Spencer Finch, entitled *Trying To Remember the Color of the Sky on That September Morning*, features 2,983 squares – one for each of the 2001 and 1993 terrorist attack victims, and each in its own shade of blue. You are dwarfed before a sea of cobalt, azure, and turquoise. So poignant is the work that Pope Francis visited the wall on a brief tour here in 2015.

Even more poignant is what's behind the wall. There is the repository for as yet unidentified remains of 9/11 victims, operated by the Chief Medical Examiner of the City of New York. Identifications continue to be made even to this day. The repository is separate from the public space and only accessible by Medical Examiner staff. Alongside, a special Reflection Room serves as a private space reserved exclusively for 9/11 family members.

Crowning the hall is a line from an ancient Roman poem by Virgil, "No Day Shall Erase You From The Memory of Time." Each letter was forged from pieces of recovered World Trade Center steel. The transformative power of words and our collective remembrance are captured in this most sacred space.

NO DAY SHALL ERASE YOU FROM THE MEMORY OF TIME

Virgil

**Address** 180 Greenwich Street, New York, NY 10007, +1 (212)312-8800, www.911memorial.org | **Getting there** Subway to Chambers Street (A, C, 1, 2, 3), Fulton Street (A, C, J, 2, 3, 4, 5), Park Place (2, 3), Cortlandt Street (R), Rector Street (1) | **Hours** Sun–Thu 9am–8pm, Fri & Sat 9am–9pm | **Tip** Stand in awe of the 9/11 Survivor Tree, a Callery pear tree that was burned and broken in the attack, nursed back to life, and is now replanted on Memorial Plaza (www.911memorial.org/survivor-tree).

# 75__Neue Galerie

*Mysteries of* The Woman in Gold

It's one of the most famous paintings in the world. The *Portrait of Adele Bloch-Bauer 1*, completed by Gustav Klimt in 1907, is a work you must see in person. Only then can you take in its shimmering, gold surface with an aura that's all its own. The beloved painting is displayed inside a paneled drawing room and is the jewel of the Neue Galerie. The collection is housed in a lavish 1914 townhouse-turned-museum and focuses on early 20th-century German and Austrian art and design. Opened in 2001 by art collector Ronald S. Lauder, the Neue Galerie is one of the city's most elegant museums, and people from all over the world make the pilgrimage here to see *The Woman in Gold*.

It's the pure radiance of the painting that astounds. Painted in oil, with silver and gold leaf, Bloch-Bauer's face is crisply rendered. Her hands are clasped beneath her chin, perhaps concealing a disfigured finger. A wealthy society woman, Adele hosted regular Viennese salons, and the portrait was commissioned by her husband, who was a Jewish banker. Her gown merges with the background into a wild swirl of triangular and oval patterns and has the sitter's initials, *AB*. Is she standing or sitting? It's hard to tell. She seems to hover, staring boldly back at us, not just earthly but divine as well.

*The Woman in Gold* is classic Klimt. Inspired by Byzantine mosaics, the Austrian artist's father was a goldsmith. Adele was his friend, and he did some 100 preparatory drawings for this work.

In 1941, the masterpiece was seized by the Nazis. The glorious choker Adele wears in the painting was taken as well. After an eight-year court battle, the Bloch-Bauer family got the painting back in 2006. Lauder then purchased it for $135 million and brought it to the museum, where it will remain always. Complete your visit with exquisite Viennese pastries in the atmospheric Café Sabarsky or Café Fledermaus on the lower level.

Address 1048 5th Avenue, New York, NY 10028, +1 (212)628-6200, www.neuegalerie.com, museum@neuegalerie.org | Getting there Subway to 86th Street/Lexington Avenue (4, 5, 6), 86th Street/Central Park West (B, C) | Hours Thu – Mon 11am – 6pm | Tip To learn more about the painting and the fight to have it returned to the family, see the 2015 movie, "Woman in Gold," starring Helen Mirren.

# 76 Nevelson Chapel of Tranquility

*The geometry of white*

With her trademark bright scarf and thick, thick false eyelashes, it must have been marvelous to come upon artist Louise Nevelson (1899–1988) in the 1960s, scrounging around the streets of Manhattan, searching for discarded scraps of wood. A chair leg here, an abandoned door there. Later, she would take the refuse to her studio, join the pieces together like a jigsaw puzzle, and paint them black or white for her iconic wall sculptures. She called them "environments."

You can see one of her most immersive environments in Midtown inside The Chapel of the Good Shepherd at Saint Peter's Church. Built in 1977, this is a quiet place of contemplation, a small space with just a handful of pews. But the six abstract wall sculptures, painted a soft white, carry a potent energy. Up close, your gaze gets lost in the undulating movement of the reliefs that feel like three-dimensional collages. Shadow and light, elliptical and oval, rectangular and square, all seemingly random shapes coalescing into a satisfying whole.

The chapel was the gift of Erol Beker, who is interred to the left of a central gold cross. And even though Nevelson herself was Jewish, she accepted this commission to create a unifying space and quiet refuge from the frenetic New York streets. She designed it when she was a well-known, outspoken artist in her late seventies who by then had graced magazine covers and had major museum exhibitions.

Some 40 years later, the diminutive chapel remains as popular as ever with frequent visitors from the bustling Citigroup Center building next door. But all that use has created conservation issues, and for years the paint has been flaking from the walls, and parts of the wood are damaged. An extensive restoration is underway to save the chapel, with a rigorous three-phase plan. As Nevelson liked to say, "True strength is delicate."

Address 619 Lexington Avenue, New York, NY 10022, +1 (212)935-2200,
www.nevelsonchapel.org | Hours Daily 8am–8pm | Tip Saint Peters is known as the jazz
church. Check the website for midday concerts and jazz services featuring top notch
musicians (619 Lexington Avenue, New York, NY 10022, www.saintpeters.org/jazz).

# 77 __ New Museum

*Where the new is now*

From the outside, this striking architectural silhouette on the Bowery appears to be a giant stack of shifting metal boxes. But it's this museum's 'out of the box' approach to art that is both cutting edge and cool. Think of it as a museum mixed with an alternative art space, always embracing the new but with a curatorial eye.

The location itself is key. Right in the heart of the Lower East Side art gallery scene, the New Museum lives up to its name as a global touchstone for 21st-century art. They take chances here with a schedule of exhibitions that are fresh and fearless showing art that at first makes you scratch your head and later realize its importance.

Examples include the exhibition, "The Keeper," where the idea of obsessive collecting was fleshed out and filled the museum with 3,000 family album photos of people posing with teddy bears, all collected by one woman. Or the Pixel Forest exhibition by Swiss artist Pipilotti Rist (see ch. 54), with its immersive video, light, and music environments that transported visitors into an imaginary world. Works at this museum can swing between the glorious, the curious, and the confusing. And that's their mission: to hold a mirror up to today's artists and reflect it back to all of us. Pushing boundaries is part of the plan.

Especially strong is the museum's extensive Digital Archive, a living diary of the institution. You can access thousands of images and videos, including exhibitions, performances, and artist interviews. And while the Whitney Museum has the famed Biennial exhibition for American art, the New Museum hosts the Triennial, a sampling of the best new art from around the world.

Don't miss the New Museum Store, a highly original shop inside the light-filled lobby. You can find cheeky snow globes, clocks, coasters, and bags sometimes designed by the very artists shown in the museum.

**Address** 235 Bowery, New York, NY 10002, +1 (212)219-1222, www.newmuseum.org, info@newmuseum.org | **Getting there** Subway to Broadway-Lafayette Street (B, D, F, M), Prince Street (R, W), Spring Street (6), Bowery (J) | **Hours** Tue & Wed, Fri–Sun 11am–6pm, Thu 11am–9pm | **Tip** Explore the dozens of Lower East Side art galleries around the museum (www.lesgallerymap.com).

# 78 New York City Fire Museum
*A bravery that burns brightly*

This small, artfully curated museum is a complete aesthetic surprise. Housed in a Beaux Arts 1904 former firehouse, the New York City Fire Museum is where you'd expect to discover the hard work and heroics of NYC's firefighters. But you will be surprised and delighted by the displays of paintings, uniforms, and ceremonial objects that underscore the romance and pageantry of the firefighting community.

In a densely packed city like New York, a fearless fire department is essential. Learn about the bucket brigades that were the beginnings of the department. On view is a series of leather buckets that were actually made by shoemakers. Homeowners' names and addresses are painted on the buckets. Nearby, an 1875 hand-pulled hose reel shows how the volunteer firefighters took pride in their rigs, decorating them richly with torches and plumes of feathers. Then finally, we see parade capes, painted ceremonial helmets, and presentation trumpets.

The dangers of the job are also represented. Inside a glass vitrine is a rare, 1935 Ambulance Last Rites Kit, a sobering reminder of the profession's great perils. The portable box contains two candles and brass candlesticks, holy water, and a priest's stole and prayer book. There is also a special room devoted entirely to the 343 members of the FDNY who lost their lives on September 11, 2001. The solemn, sky-lit space holds a touching memorial for the firefighters, along with items from the Ground Zero recovery effort.

The "FDNY of Today" exhibit is highlighted with videos, artifacts, and bright red fire rigs. Even the small pieces of equipment make a big impact, like the partially burned life-saving rope used to rescue a man from a 2016 fire on the Upper East Side. You can also try on real firefighting jackets and helmets so you can literally feel the weight the firefighters carry on their shoulders.

Address 278 Spring Street, New York, NY 10013, +1 (212)691-1303, www.nycfiremuseum.org, info@nycfiremuseum.org | Getting there Subway to Spring Street (C, E), Houston Street (1) | Hours Daily 10am–5pm | Tip See what's playing at the SoHo Playhouse. From fringe to fabulous, it's one of the city's oldest off-Broadway venues (15 Vandam Street, New York, NY 10013, www.sohoplayhouse.com).

# 79___New York Earth Room
*Down and dirty*

This space on the second floor of a classic SoHo building may not be what you expect. The scent hits you first – moist earth, like a freshly planted garden. Turn the corner, and there it is: an otherwise empty white loft space filled wall to wall with black dirt. Just dirt. Nothing else. Stand there and quietly take it in. The work reveals itself in time.

Created in 1977 by Walter De Maria (1935–2013), this museum contains one of the minimalist earth sculptures for which the artist became known. The dirt is piled knee high, 250 cubic yards spread out evenly across the floor. It fills 3,600 square feet and weighs 280,000 pounds. At first you aren't sure what to think. Light streams in from broad windows, casting shadows. The sight. The smell. The utter quiet. And then perhaps, memories filter in. Walking in the forest, planting tomatoes, passing a farm field. It's the sheer simplicity that allows private thoughts to come through. And before you know it, you are transported somewhere else, far away from this New York City loft.

Run by the Dia Art Foundation, the work's caretaker is Bill Dilworth, who has been watching over the very same dirt for more than 30 years. Wearing knee-high boots, he waters and rakes the soil once a week. "The light is always changing here," Dilworth says, "and it gets blue-ish right before sunset." The nearby *Broken Kilometer* (see ch. 10) is also by De Maria.

Word of mouth is how most people find this art space. And once here, you are likely to have the room to yourself. It's a perfect refuge, although there have been regular visitors over the years. "There was this guy who came in once a day. He was working at a job nearby and became obsessed," Dilworth recalls. Perhaps that is the power of the Earth Room. It's different for everyone. And each time you visit, you are free to wander in your mind, wherever the space takes you.

Address 141 Wooster Street, New York, NY 10012, +1 (212)989-5566, www.diaart.org | Getting there Subway to Prince Street (R, W), Broadway-Lafayette (B, D, F, M), Spring Street (C, E), Bleecker Street (6), Houston Street (1) | Hours Sept–June, Wed–Sun noon–6pm (closed 3–3:30pm); see website for seasonal dates | Tip With its blooming borders and eclectic garden statuary, the Elizabeth Street Garden feels like a secret treasure you've just stumbled upon. It is perfectly charming (Elizabeth Street, between Prince & Spring Streets, www.elizabethstreetgarden.com).

# Dia Art Foundation
# Walter De Maria
# The New York Earth Room, 1977

# 80__New York Public Library Map Room

*Explore the world in a scroll arm chair*

Think of the main branch of the New York Public Library's exquisite Schwarzman Building as an elaborate museum. With its wonderfully grand Beaux Arts architecture and massive collection of books and artifacts, this library is part of the city's fabric, character, and intellect. It is also an exciting place to see some of the liveliest and most memorable exhibitions in town.

While the exhibits change regularly, there is one room in the library that does not. The diminutive, jewel-like Map Room is a dreamy space where you can explore the world while sitting in a wooden scroll arm chair. Up above, the ornamented and gilded ceiling is as detailed as a Fabergé egg. The room is further decorated with bronze chandeliers, walnut paneling, and gray marble. You will see rows and rows of books, atlases, and decorative globes. It's the ultimate retreat for library lovers.

Using the power of your library card, you can examine the most wondrous things in this room. Scan the digitalized offerings and fill out a little piece of paper, and the affable librarians will bring out your requested material. You might want to look at a rendering of the Americas from 1573, or a hand-drawn map from the American Civil War. Gently leaf through leather-tooled volumes with lavishly colored illustrations, so massive that you have to stand up to turn the textured pages. These are incredibly rare documents, and they are available for you to study.

Part of the intrigue here is the names of mysterious places on the maps: Tova, La Emperadada, Antananarivo. And part is the bird's-eye view of mountains, oceans, and islands. Illustrated volumes are adorned with ships at sea, cherubs, satyrs, and family crests. The link to history is tangible in this room.

Address 476 5th Avenue, New York, NY 10018, +1 (212)340-0863, www.nypl.org | Getting there Subway to Grand Central/42nd Street (4, 5, 6), 42nd Street/Bryant Park (B, D, F, M), Times Square/42nd Street (N, Q, R, W) | Hours Sun 10am–5pm, Mon & Thu 8am–8pm, Tue & Wed 8am–9pm, Fri 8am–6pm, Sat 10am–6pm | Tip On your way out, don't forget to say a quick hello to Patience and Fortitude, the iconic pair of lions, carved from pink Tennessee marble, that have been standing guard since 1911.

# 81 New York Public Library for the Performing Arts

*Bernstein, Broadway, and Beatlemania*

For many New Yorkers, Lincoln Center is the artistic heart of the city, an island of culture where the Metropolitan Opera, New York City Ballet, and New York Philharmonic all come together around a shimmering fountain. Hidden off to the right of the Opera House is the New York Public Library for the Performing Arts, featuring fascinating exhibits. Few experiences are lovelier than spending hours engrossed in art, beauty, history, and wonder.

This library is a grand journey of discovery into the heart and soul of Lincoln Center. As you enter through front doors, you'll see small windows to the left. You've found toe shoe central. A pink pointe shoe is beautifully autographed by Russian dancer Alexandra Danilova. More windows hold more toe shoes signed by iconic ballerinas, who go through at least one pair of shoes per performance. This is your satin slipper prelude.

Next, head to the gallery up ahead, where rotating exhibitions offer insights into the world of dance, theater, and music. You might see a tribute to American conductor Leonard Bernstein, or hear rich tunes by Gershwin filling the room. We see Bernstein's monogrammed black slippers and silver cigarette box, and even a recreation of his composing studio. Beatlemania has been featured here too, with letters, posters, and instruments from the Fab Five, along with an oral history booth where visitors could record their own Beatles stories. The library has explored themes from modern dance pioneers to Shakespeare plays.

Finally, don't miss the third floor, a theater lover's dream. It's an archive of the performing arts at your fingertips, with videos of hundreds of ballet and Broadway performances, past and present. You can sit and watch Suzanne Farrell on pointe or Patti LuPone on stage. The selections are endless.

Address 40 Lincoln Center Plaza, New York, NY 10023, +1 (917)275-6975, www.nypl.org |
Getting there Subway to West 66 Street/Lincoln Center (1); bus to Broadway/West 66th
Street (M5), Columbus Avenue/West 66th Street (M7), Central Park West/West 66th
Street (M10), Amsterdam Avenue/West 67th Street (M11) | Hours Mon 10:30am–8pm,
Tue–Sat 10:30am–6pm | Tip Enjoy one of the free concerts at the world famous Juilliard
School. You may hear jazz, classical, or anything in between (60 Lincoln Center Plaza, New
York, NY 10023, www.juilliard.edu/stage-beyond/performance-calendar).

# 82 New York Society Library

*In card catalog heaven*

Step into the grand, Italianate townhouse on the Upper East Side, and you instantly feel the intellectual history here. Founded in 1754, the posh New York Society Library remains private, but sections of it are open to everyone. Go straight ahead to the front desk, where the attendant will ask you to sign a visitor's guestbook. "Certain things here, we still do on paper," he muses. Old school indeed.

Long before public libraries were formed, this was the place to find books. George Washington was a member, as were Herman Melville and Truman Capote. You are in good company. Climb the grand staircase to the second floor, where marble sculptures of maidens and vintage oil paintings adorn the space. Up ahead on the wood-paneled landing, you'll discover small but well thought out exhibitions on books, writers, and literature. Don't expect flashy, computer-generated imagery here. It's simply a handful of vintage display cases filled with very special books and objects. You might learn about the Manhattan life of Willa Cather, enjoy writings about gardening, or have a look at Edith Wharton's New York. These exhibits may not make the headlines, but they are carefully curated displays that quietly delight and educate in the most wonderful, classic ways.

Take the exquisite, paneled elevator down to the ground floor and enter the Reference Room, where you will find an ornate fireplace, worn wooden chairs, and a tooled leather-top table – and one of the city's greatest hidden treasures. The immense card catalog spans an entire wall. It is a small museum in and of itself. Open one of the wooden drawers by its curled brass pull. Inside, carefully typewritten cards carry the names of thousands of books found in the stacks. You can feel the age of the cards, some yellowed with time. Take a good whiff too; it's the unmistakable scent of old libraries.

Address 53 East 79th Street, New York, NY 10075, +1 (212)288-6900, www.nysoclib.org, reference@nysoclib.org | Getting there Subway to 77th Street (6), 81st Street/Museum of Natural History (B, C), 86th Street (4,5, N, Q) | Hours Mon & Fri 9am–5pm, Tue–Thu 9am–8pm, Sat & Sun 11am–5pm | Tip Stroll over to Central Park to see the delightful bronze statue of Alice in Wonderland, the Mad Hatter, and the White Rabbit. Children have been polishing the patina since 1959 (East 74th Street, New York, NY 10021).

# 83  New York Transit Museum

*The art of the underground*

From the outside, this Brooklyn subway entrance looks like any other. But it's not. It's really an underground museum, where you can discover the nostalgic side of Big Apple transit. Located inside the decommissioned Court Street subway station, the New York Transit Museum has two levels to explore. It's the kind of place little kids love to discover. And if you look closely, you'll see small design elements of New York City travel: the artful side of the subway.

Begin on the lower-level platform, where you'll find a fleet of vintage train cars. Step on board. The oldest, a 1907 wooden car, looks a bit cabin-like, painted a rustic brown. Inside, you'll discover the very handsome rattan covered seats, with their basket-like weave. Made from woven reeds, rattan was an inexpensive and durable form of upholstery. And yet to the modern eye, it looks fancy. Vintage advertisements line the train walls and immerse you in the period, like an image of a luscious strawberry shortcake for Royal Baking Powder. Then don't miss the 1949 Million Dollar Train, so called because of the hefty price tag when ten of these cars were purchased. Lively spring green, with apple-red floors, the stainless-steel car features round porthole windows, like something out of a Hitchcock movie.

The ceramic arts are well-represented here, with vintage, terra-cotta plaques designed and produced to make subway stops beautiful and distinctive. We see the 50th Street plaque, manufactured in 1904 by the iconic Grueby Faience Company. It features their trademark matte green glaze, modeled in an Arts and Crafts aesthetic.

Then finally, we see a mini exhibition of specially commissioned subway art. Beginning in 1991, the city selected artists to design posters for the train cars, illustrating favorite destinations, like peacocks for the Bronx Zoo and lively scenes from Times Square.

Address 99 Schermerhorn Street, Brooklyn, NY 11201, +1 (728)694-1600 | Getting there Subway to Borough Hall (2, 3, 4, 5), Jay Street/Metrotech (A, C, F), Hoyt-Schermerhorn Streets (G) | Hours Tue–Fri 10am–4pm, Sat & Sun 11am–5pm | Tip Once settled by Dutch farmers, quaint Cobble Hill Park nearby is a peaceful place to go for a stroll (Clinton Street, between Congress Street & Verandah Place, Brooklyn, NY 11201, www.nycgovparks.org/parks/cobble-hill-park).

# 84 New York Yankees Museum

*Take me out to the ball game*

Go behind the iconic pinstripes at this museum located inside Yankee Stadium, where it's all about bats, balls, and baseball bling. "With this team, our history is our identity," says museum curator Brian Richards. Open for ticket holders on game days and during guided tours, The New York Yankees Museum is a quick run around the bases with much to see.

Front and center, two life-sized statues show pitcher Don Larsen throwing an imaginary ball to catcher Yogi Berra. Commemorating Larsen's legendary 'perfect game' during the 1956 World Series, the statues stand a regulation 60 feet, 6 inches apart. And in between them sits a long glass case with 870 baseballs signed by the greats: Babe Ruth, Mickey Mantle, and Derek Jeter. The wall of white baseballs, seemingly floating in air, is an aesthetic home run.

Next, glistening in gold, are not one, but seven Yankees World Series trophies on display. We see the earlier, more elaborate trophies, with a large gold crown in the center. Then from 2000 on, Tiffany & Co. began making the trophies, paring down the design to a ring of flags; one for each Major League team. Nearby there's more jewelry in a case of World Series rings. Made by Balfour, the 1940s examples are simple and elegant. But by 1999, the modern designs look downright dangerous. Heavily encrusted in ornament, the jeweled knuckledusters must be a work-out to wear.

Ultimately, it's all about the pinstripes, with some iconic uniforms worn by Babe Ruth and Lou Gehrig – woolen wonders long before the moisture wicking fabrics of today. "Oh yes, they were extremely hot to wear," Richards says. Look for the prized notched bat used by Babe Ruth during the 1927–1928 season. Each time Ruth homered, he made a little notch, carving 11 notches for 11 home runs.

Address 1 East 161st Street, Bronx, NY 10451, +1 (718)293-4300, www.mlb.com/ yankees | Getting there Subway to 161st Street/Yankee Stadium (4, B, D) | Hours Open for ticket holders on game days | Tip Visit Yankee Stadium's Monument Park, with a collection of plaques, monuments, and retired numbers of Yankees greats. See website for details (www.mlb.com/yankees).

# 85 New-York Historical Society

*A stairway to Tiffany heaven*

Wandering into the dramatically lit, jewel-like Gallery of Tiffany Lamps at the New-York Historical Society is an escape into a glistening, glass wonderland. Be prepared for true beauty. One hundred of the museum's vintage Tiffany lamps are on view in this gallery's two floors that are connected by a floating, lighted, glass staircase. The effect is dazzling.

Louis Comfort Tiffany (1848–1933) pioneered these icons of early 20th-century design at a time when the incandescent bulb was brand new. These artful shades softened the light and added panache. But it's the nature-based designs that collectors clamored for, and many of these classic styles are here to see up close. The beloved Wisteria lamp, with its thicket of sinuous vines, positively glows. Nearby, is the lovely Dragonfly design, delicate in every way. And look for the elaborate Cobweb shade on a Narcissus mosaic base, a rare sight. It was Tiffany who developed new kinds of glass in the years around 1900, allowing for these designs to flourish. And here amidst the azure blue walls and curved glass cases, the lamps look better than ever.

But Tiffany did not design alone. You'll also learn about the so-called Tiffany Girls of the Women's Glass Cutting Department, whom Tiffany Studios employed to create these treasures. Led by the talented Clara Driscoll (1861–1944), these women have a hidden history that the New-York Historical Society helped uncover. The women worked in anonymity at the time, but you can see photos of every woman in the group, whom we now celebrate all these years later.

You'll also get a chance to design your own imaginary Tiffany lamp with an interactive digital display. Choose a color, design, style, and base. Then see it virtually materialize before your eyes. See if you can tell the real Tiffany lamp from the fake on display.

Address 170 Central Park West, New York, NY 10024, +1 (212)873-3400, www.nyhistory.org, info@nyhistory.org | Getting there Subway to 81st Street (B, C), 79th Street (1) | Hours Tue–Thu & Sat 10am–6pm, Fri 10am–8pm, Sat 10am–6pm, Sun 11am–5pm | Tip The nearby Dakota is one of the most famous residences in Manhattan. An architectural treasure, it is also the spot where John Lennon was shot to death in 1980 (1 West 72nd Street, New York, NY 10023).

# 86 Nicholas Roerich Museum

*A lost paradise on the Upper West Side*

This may be the most jam-packed, one-man museum in New York City. And it's filled with works by an artist you've probably never heard of, which is exactly why it's so captivating. Find your way to the far end of West 107th Street, which is perched on a hill above Riverside Drive. Lined with swoon-worthy Beaux Arts townhomes, the neighborhood feels more like a European village. There's a faded plaque at number 319. Push open the arched, wooden doorway, and you've arrived.

Born in Russia, but painting mostly in the Himalayas, mystical artist Nicholas Roerich (1874–1947) created paintings that sell for millions of dollars today. But even on this very street, many New Yorkers don't know his work. Climb the wooden stairway to the second floor, with its stained-glass windows and ornate fireplaces. Though the space is sparsely furnished, it is filled with vivid paintings that astound – two entire floors, room after room, one painting on top of another. You are immersed in the brightly colored world of the master. Steely blue mountains. Winding paths to infinity. Night skies. This museum is a utopian, painterly place that transports you to another realm.

"The works are especially bright because he painted in tempera," gallery assistant Katrina Dessavre says. "It dried more quickly, and he liked that the pigment would fade over time." Roerich painted 7,000 works, and some 200 are here. But he was also a poet, philosopher, and peace activist, a costume and set designer, and political advisor. A planet was named after him. And he was nominated for the Nobel Peace Prize in 1929 for his efforts to protect works of art during the war. All that, and still Americans don't know him.

We see a self-portrait of the artist, long white beard, lost in thought. You wonder what he would have made of this little museum hidden on a quiet street, keeping his legacy alive.

Address 319 West 107th Street, New York, NY 10025, +1 (212)864-7752, www.roerich.org, inquiries@roerich.org | Getting there Subway to Cathedral Parkway/ 110th Street (1); bus to Riverside Drive/West 108th Street (M 5), Broadway/West 108th Street (M 104), West 106th Street/Broadway (M 116) | Hours Tue–Fri noon–4pm, Sat & Sun 2–5pm | Tip On the same block, don't miss the nearby residence at number 303. It is an extremely narrow sliver-of-a-townhouse that looks like something out of a fairy tale (303 West 107th Street, New York, NY 10025).

# 87__The Noguchi Museum

*An oasis of calm*

It's rare to enter a museum that was designed and installed by the artist himself and filled with his iconic works, often placed exactly where he wanted them. But that's the case at the Noguchi Museum in Long Island City. It's as if the spirit of the sculptor is guiding you along the display of his iconic works. One of the leading sculptors and designers of the 20th century, Japanese-American Isamu Noguchi (1904–1988) established a studio in the neighborhood in the 1960s. He later purchased this 1920s industrial building across the street from his studio to show his life's work and build a space of quiet reflection.

To begin, enter the open-air, cinder block building that was once a small gas station. Fresh air filters in, and sinewy birch trees bring nature indoors. Large basalt sculptures look like looming personages. In the polished and oxidized surfaces, you see the hand of nature and of the sculptor. There is a blending of East and West, traditional and modern. These are some of the tensions Noguchi played with throughout his life.

Inside, the white, windowed galleries, the feel is spare and simple. The placement of the works is important, often infused with a sense of poetry. One large work might dominate, while smaller sculptures appear randomly set on the floor. You may notice the artist's bio-morphic aesthetic, where works sometimes appear abstract and yet somehow human at the same time. "The best is that which is most spontaneous or seemingly so," Noguchi said of his ceramic works.

That ease of placement extends to an outdoor sculpture garden, which fuses form, nature, and neighborhood. It's the perfect place to reflect on the works all around. In the giftshop finally, we see Noguchi the designer in his iconic Akari light sculptures. Made from handmade washi paper with bamboo ribbing, the lanterns glow from within. They are considered icons of 1950's modern design.

Address 9-01 33rd Road, Queens, NY 11106, +1 (718)204-7088, www.noguchi.org, info@noguchi.org | Getting there Subway to 21st Street–Queensbridge (F), Vernon Boulevard–Jackson Avenue (7), NYC Ferry to Astoria | Hours Wed–Fri 10am–5pm, Sat & Sun 11am–6pm | Tip See Noguchi's large, iconic *Red Cube* (1968), a site-specific outdoor sculpture in Lower Manhattan (140 Broadway, New York, NY 10005, www.noguchi.org/noguchi/works/red-cube).

# 88 Paley Center for Media

*Escape to television nirvana*

Think of the Paley Center as the ultimate destination for couch potatoes, where you can binge-watch favorite television programs to your heart's content. All that's missing is the couch. Right in the shadow of the looming CBS broadcast building on 52nd Street, the center was established in 1975 by the network's broadcast pioneer William S. Paley. Because television is on a continuous, ever-changing path, the idea was to create a place where programming can live on forever.

Ride the elevator to the fourth floor, where a librarian will greet you at the door and then help get you started. You'll take a seat at one of the 40-some viewing stations, which are bathed in darkness. Put your headphones on, log into the computer, and there at your fingertips are over 160,000 viewing and listening options. The choices are staggering. You can select everything from the 1960 Kennedy-Nixon debate, to the 1969 moon landing, to *All in the Family* episodes. There are documentaries, news broadcasts, and dance performances. TV programs like *The Waltons*, *Thirtysomething*, or the 1970s PBS drama *An American Family*. All eras, all genres, high and low culture. You think you'll spend about 30 minutes here, but before you know, it's been an hour and a half. The room is completely silent, except for the occasional person chuckling out loud. You are among kindred spirits.

Perhaps most striking are the old black-and-white commercials that show the very earliest advertising campaigns. You'll see dancing packs of cigarettes, like the Lucky Strike cigarette barn dance, or the tap-dancing Old Gold cigars. Equally amusing are Budweiser beer commercials with sayings like, "Where There's Life, There's Bud." They are signposts of how Americans lived, who they admired, what they longed for. In this small room, the vast world of television is laid out before us. We thank you, Mr. Paley.

Address 25 West 52nd Street, New York, NY 10019, +1 (212)621-6600,
www.paleycenter.org, info@paleycenter.org | Getting there Subway to 5th Avenue/
53rd Street (E, M), 47-50th Street/Rockefeller Center (B, D, F, M), 51st Street (6),
50th Street (1) | Hours Wed, Fri – Sun noon – 6pm, Thu noon – 8pm | Tip Stop by
St. Thomas Church to see their elaborate stained-glass windows, recently restored.
The window of Christ as a boy is a treasure (1 West 53rd Street, New York, NY 10019,
www.saintthomaschurch.org).

# 89 __ Park Avenue Armory
*Gilded Age grandeur*

It's one of the most extraordinary rooms in New York City, and yet it's hidden away inside an armory. The Veterans Room is a tour de force of shimmering tiles, carved woodwork, and immense iron chandeliers. This room, along with the library next door, are the only fully intact interiors in the world designed by Louis C. Tiffany, Associated Artists. Back in 1881, this young group was headed by designer Louis Comfort Tiffany and architect Stanford White. You can see their remarkable work up close on private tours.

This is not your average ammunition depot. The Seventh Regiment was the only privately funded armory in the US. It became known as the Silk Stocking regiment because of the elite group who belonged – names like Vanderbilt, Roosevelt, and Harriman. These prominent families were building grand homes nearby, and they lavished equal attention on the armory, employing the same innovative artisans and builders.

Room after room, there are touches of the Aesthetic Movement throughout, with an emphasis on the handcrafted and the exotic. Built as a military facility and a social club, the opulent reception spaces were meant for reading and taking tea. But the Veterans Room is the rare jewel. Every inch is filled with embellishment and beauty. Azure and cobalt tiles frame the fireplace, forming a sea of blue, reflecting the colors of the ocean. It was designed by Tiffany, who was barely 30 years old at the time. Then known more for his landscape paintings, he worked on the Armory before he began making stained-glass lamps.

The room's architect was even younger. Stanford White was in his twenties and had just joined the firm McKim, Mead & White. He infused the space with perfect proportions and filled it with scrolled iron work. There are Celtic knots, Chinese dragons, and Persian patterns. The Armory is a hidden masterpiece of military magnificence.

Address 643 Park Avenue, New York, NY 10065, +1 (212)616-3930, www.armoryonpark.org, info@armoryonpark.org | Getting there Subway to 68th Street/Hunter College (6), 63rd Street/Lexington Avenue (F, Q) | Hours By private tour only; see website for details | Tip With an eclectic mix of live performances, the Kaye Playhouse at Hunter College offers performances by the likes of Phillip Glass and Audra MacDonald. Check the schedule to see what's playing (695 Park Avenue, New York, NY 10065, www.hunter.cuny.edu/kayeplayhouse/history-of-the-kaye).

# 90 Queens Museum

*World's Fairs on display*

To visit the Queens Museum is to see the wonders of the World's Fair. Not one, but two World's Fairs were held on this very spot in 1939 and 1964. So it's no surprise that the museum owns some 10,000 objects related to those iconic expositions. And you can peruse some of the highlights at a little-known gallery here. It's the World's Fair Visible Storage, where you can see trinkets and treasures brought out of storage for you to enjoy and maybe even reminisce.

The legendary – and controversial – developer Robert Moses was the man who turned an ash dump in this area into the site of both World's Fairs. We see Moses' IBM Selectric typewriter, the picture of modernity at the time. Also on view, a white telephone from his desk. On April 21, 1963, Moses received a call from President Kennedy on this very phone, to signal the one-year countdown to the fair's opening. Sadly, Kennedy was assassinated seven months later.

Rather than Pavilions of Nations, in the spirit of American commerce, many of the pavilions were created by private companies. The 1939 World's Fair's Futurama exhibit at the General Motors Pavilion was all the rage, with its predictions of massive highways in the future. We see an actual floor from the display, along with little cars and human figures. That same year, Con Edison had a City of Light Pavilion, with models of the Coney Island Wonder Wheel and a New York City subway car, also on display. Dotted throughout the cases are fair-themed souvenirs: vintage plates, jewelry, and figurines.

But the biggest World's Fair trinket is just outside the museum. It's the impressive, gargantuan, stainless-steel globe called the Unisphere. Built by a division of US Steel to symbolize the beginning of the Space Age, it was the centerpiece of the 1964 World's Fair. There's a great view of the Unisphere from the museum's upper-floor windows.

**Address** New York City Building, Flushing Meadows Corona Park, Queens, NY 11368, +1 (718)592-9700, www.queensmuseum.org, info@queensmuseum.org | **Getting there** Subway to Mets-Willets Point (7); bus to 108th Street/Corona Avenue (Q23), Roosevelt Avenue/Grand Central Parkway (Q48) | **Hours** Wed – Sun 11am – 5pm | **Tip** Look for the statue of tennis champion and AIDS activist Arthur Ashe at the nearby USTA Billie Jean King National Tennis Center, which hosts the US Open every August (Flushing Meadows–Corona Park, Flushing, NY 11368, www.ustanew2.gotennissource.com).

# 91_Red Hook Wooden Barge Museum

*A floating collection of curiosities*

"Welcome aboard," the affable Captain David Sharps chirps, with a little bow from the waist. "There's a lot to see." There certainly is. Docked along a quiet corner in Brooklyn's Red Hook neighborhood, this 100-year-old floating barge is a museum, art gallery, theater, and family home, all rolled into one. With views of the Statue of Liberty right outside the door, this private world is like no other.

"It's a way of combining my love of the arts with my love of old things," Sharps tells visitors. With worn wooden floors below and sculptural skylights above, hundreds of vintage seafaring objects fill every corner – hand-painted wooden signs, walls of glass lanterns, stacks of circular life rafts, tables of wooden buoys. There are paintings of ships at sea and photos of boats in port. There is even a kinetic sound sculpture, with a ball that makes synchronized bell and xylophone sounds. It's a bit like a quirky Parisian atelier full of curiosities.

As it turns out, Sharps once lived on a barge docked on the Seine in Paris, while studying to be a mime. Most of his life he's worked as a clown and a juggler. But in 1986, when he spotted the Lehigh Valley Barge No. 79 mired in the mud in New Jersey, he had to have it. It's the last remaining vessel of its kind, now turned into a floating museum on the history of New York's waterfront. "Voila," the captain extols, unfurling a painted theater backdrop. In an instant, he's converted the barge into a showboat, where he hosts plays, concerts, and art exhibitions. Even a Pirates Ball. It's the ultimate Brooklyn hangout.

Check out the adjoining galley, or kitchen, actually used by Sharps, his wife, and two children, who have lived here full-time. Roaring fire, aged oriental carpets, vintage wooden table on wheels – the rustic elegance is cozy and inviting. You'll want to move right into this site-specific, floating museum.

Address 290 Conover Street, Brooklyn, NY 11231, +1 (718)624-4719, www.waterfrontmuseum.org | **Getting there** Bus to Beard Street/Van Brunt Street (B 61), Beard/Otsego Streets (B 57) | **Hours** Sat 1–5pm, Thu 4–8pm | **Tip** For even closer views of the Statue of Liberty, visit the charming, waterside Valentino Pier, where young families picnic on the grass, and fishermen cast lines into the water. It's one of the city's hidden parks (Ferris & Coffey Streets, Brooklyn, NY 11231, www.nycgovparks.org).

# 92__Rose Museum
### *Getting to Carnegie Hall*

It's amazing what treasures are forgotten and waiting to be found again. In the early 1990s, Director of Archives Gino Francesconi was looking for objects to put in a little museum at Carnegie Hall, when he got a call from Benny Goodman's daughter. If he could display it, she was willing to donate one of her father's clarinets. "The answer was yes," Francesconi recalled. "Then, because of that, someone called and said, 'I have Gene Krupa's drumsticks.' And it just blossomed from there."

Those pieces on display just off the main stage tell the story of one of the most famous concert halls in the world. Trimmed with exotic African wood, inspired by the wood on a violin, the one-room museum is filled with surprises. The Beatles played two concerts here on their first American trip in 1964. With all the excitement, Paul McCartney's name was listed as 'John McCartney' on the program. You can see the amusing typo here, where McCartney actually signed his real name over the error. Nearby, is an exquisitely patterned scarf used by Isadora Duncan when she danced here in 1910. Her brother Raymond Duncan designed the scarf, and his name is stamped on it. "That piece is extremely rare," Francesconi confides.

But of course it's the classical music world here that shines. On view is the very first program from when the hall opened in 1891. Tchaikovsky arrived to conduct and caused a sensation wherever he went, writing in his diary, "Everywhere, I am besieged with autograph seekers." We see one of his signatures before us, alongside a musical notation. Nearby is a piece of the old wood stage, with a curious nail pounded in it marking the exact spot to place the piano for a famous 1968 televised concert by Vladimir Horowitz.

Pair the museum with a guided tour of the famed hall, and you can see the legendary stage from a performer's perspective.

Address 154 West 57th Street, New York, NY 10019, www.carnegiehall.org/About/
Building-Overview/Rose-Museum | Getting there Subway to 59th Street/Columbus
Circle (1, A, B, C, D), 57th Street/Seventh Avenue (N, Q, R, W), 57th Street/
6th Avenue (F) | Hours Daily, Sept 17–July 22 11am–4:30pm | Tip See the massive,
cherry red *Love Sculpture* by artist Robert Indiana; poised on a busy midtown corner. It
always attracts crowds with its Pop Art playfulness (West 55th Street & 6th Avenue,
New York, NY 10019).

# 93 __ Rubin Museum of Art

*Inside a sacred space*

Right in the heart of Chelsea, there's a hidden temple of tranquility that instantly transports you to another plane. It's inside the Rubin Museum of Art, up on the fourth floor, tucked away in a quiet corner. The tranquil Tibetan Buddhist Shrine Room is an ode to stillness. What they've created here is the kind of private shrine you might find in an affluent Himalayan home. Candles flicker. The faint smell of incense wafts by. You are content to just… be.

It's the visual splendor here that is arresting. Some 100 objects are precisely arranged in a colorful, glistening tableau that appeals to all the senses. For sight, an urn-shaped butter lamp offers enlightenment. It would traditionally burn clarified butter, or ghee, which is also an ingredient in traditional foods. The idea of sound comes alive with metal cymbals played on the fingertips for touch. And for scent, a pair of hammered metal incense vessels feature lion heads and intricately pierced tops. Representing purification, the vessels were often carried in pairs, during processions.

All of these objects are framed by a temple-like, painted, wooden cabinet. Gilt-copper Buddha and Bodhisattva statues, the most sacred of Tibetan Buddhist symbols, are set into its carved niches. Placed around the shrine are colorful paintings on fabric to add vibrant detail and so much visual beauty. Standing in this environment, you quickly understand how art and objects are essential to this devotional practice.

Let this mindset guide you as you wander through the galleries. The rest of the museum is just as thoughtfully assembled with exhibitions on traditional and contemporary Himalayan art. Grounded by a central, curved staircase, galleries are small and intimate, offering up-close examinations of paintings, textiles, drawings, and everyday objects. Even just a half hour here calms the mind and allows you to step away from the outside world.

Address 150 West 17th Street, New York, NY 10011, +1 (212)620-5000, www.rubinmuseum.org, info@rubinmuseum.org | Getting there Subway to 14th Street (A, C, E, F, L, M, 2, 3), or 18th Street (1) | Hours Mon & Thu 11am–5pm, Wed 11am–9pm, Fri 11am–10pm, Sat & Sun 11am–6pm | Tip To see more Tibetan and Himalayan art, take the famous Staten Island ferry over to visit the Jacques Marchais Museum of Tibetan Art (338 Lighthouse Avenue, Staten Island, NY 10306, www.tibetanmuseum.org).

# 94 Scandinavia House

*A smorgasbord of fun*

It's easy to love a cultural institution that holds a regular Knitting Night, just one of the surprises in store at Scandinavia House Nordic Center In America. This tribute to Nordic life is parked amidst the classic brick buildings on Park Avenue. Unapologetically modern, the glass box appears to float, its loft-like floors connected with a screen-wall of aged zinc and Finnish spruce. Look up, and you'll see the colorful flags of Denmark, Finland, Iceland, Norway, and Sweden, a most cheery welcome right from the start.

Inside, the brilliance of Scandinavian art and design come alive. Simplicity, minimalism, and functionality are key. Scandinavia House is also home to a shop that sells products with a Scandinavian design ethos that everyday objects should be useful, beautiful, and made to last. It's an idea espoused by Finnish designer Tapio Wirkkala, whose Iittala rippled glassware is meant to mimic the melting ice of Lapland. Contemporary Nordic jewelry looks whisper-light, and graphic Marimekko prints delight.

A similar aesthetic frames the rotating roster of art exhibitions, which are quite splendid and timely. Look for luminous Danish seascapes, magical Nordic landscapes, and immersive, light-based journeys into the far north. Artists here may be a bit lesser known in America, and they quickly become favorites, like early 20th-century Finnish painter Helene Schjerfbeck, whose spare, penetrating portraits are haunting.

For children, the inventive Playing & Learning Center is hands-on, with a Please Touch wall and a sensory tunnel, all set within a bright, modern loft. Finally, the culinary arts come alive in the Smörgås Chef restaurant, where you can sit down to Swedish meatballs and lingonberries, Aquavit cured gravlax, and a glass of wine. Even better, pair the meal with a Scandinavian film for the ever-popular Dinner & A Movie night.

Address 58 Park Avenue, New York, NY 10016, +1 (212)779-3587, www.scandinaviahouse.org, info@amscan.org | Getting there Subway to Grand Central/42nd Street (4, 5, 6, 7, S) | Hours Mon–Sat 11am–10pm, Sun 11am–5pm (see website for Gallery hours) | Tip Plan your next big business venture at the Science, Industry and Business Library, where you can take classes and get help dreaming up your dream company (188 Madison Avenue, New York, NY 10016, www.nypl.org/locations/sibl).

# 95 Schomburg Center for Research in Black Culture

*A renaissance in Harlem*

There's always a buzz around this Harlem gathering spot, where the focus is on the experiences of people of African descent. Part of the New York Public Library, the Schomberg Center was founded in 1925, originally as the Division of Negro Literature, History and Prints, at the time of the Harlem Renaissance. And since then, it has amassed a world-class collection of more than ten million items, a treasure trove of books, documents, letters, art, artifacts, and memorabilia. Founded by the Puerto Rican-born collector and educator Arturo Alfonso Schomburg, the archives are rich and deep.

You'll find stellar exhibitons inside this red brick and glass building. The ground-floor gallery has large windows that look out onto the street, a purposeful connection between art and community. Inside they've shown the lyrically colorful works by New York-Miami based artist Firelei Báez, who explores the lives of Afro-Caribbean and Afro-Latina women in layers of text, foliage, and figuration.

The Black Power Movement has been highlighted as well. In the 1960s and 70s, it galvanized millions and was the broadest movement in African-American history. We see vintage Black is Beautiful metal buttons, an affirmation of black identity that was essential in the struggle for liberation. Also seen are written texts by Black Power artists and activists: books, pamphlets, and periodicals meant to spread the word on a local level. Protest songs fill the air, along with archival videos of speeches and marches. The experience is immersive.

The museum has also explored the colorful posters of the Black Power Movement, from psychedelic and vibrant, to stark and minimal. Rare surviving examples showed bold designs and new graphic elements. It's the power of print: created to last for a short period of time, now preserved forever (see ch. 41).

Address 515 Malcom X Boulevard, New York, NY 10037, +1 (917)275-6975, www.nypl.org/
locations/schomburg | Getting there Subway to 135th Street (2, 3), 135th Street (A),
135th Street (B) | Hours Mon, Thu – Sat 10am – 6pm, Tue & Wed 10am – 8pm | Tip See
the venerable Abyssinian Baptist Church. The 11:30am service on Sundays is open to visitors
(132 West 138th Street, New York, NY 10030, www.abyssinian.org/contact-us/visitors).

# 96 _ SculptureCenter

*Spelunking for art*

You find yourself at the end of a dead-end street in Long Island City. Over to the left, that seemingly abandoned brick building with *Derrick and Hoist Co. Inc.* emblazoned at the top is your destination. SculptureCenter is not your average, reconfigured 19th-century museum building. It's a modern, non-collecting experimental laboratory, where the idea of three-dimensional art is ushered into another dimension.

Artist and acclaimed architect Maya Lin had the good sense to renovate this former trolley repair shop, updated by Andrew Berman in 2014, while keeping its inherent grittiness intact. Exposed brick walls, giant iron beams, and pitted cement floors define the sleek first-floor gallery. Wander down to the crazy puzzle of rooms in the basement, and you'll see old water meters on the walls and winding cement tunnels. Set inside these industrial niches are cutting-edge sculptures like you've never seen before. As you explore and discover each corner, you feel as though you are rummaging through an abandoned building, with the thrill of potential danger creeping up behind you at any moment. These are not the kind of polite marble sculptures you'll find at the Met.

Many successful artists working today had their first shows here. All works rotate and have included Jon Wang's immersive video and sound environment featuring live silk worms cocooning, eating, and spinning silk threads. Live video of the silkworms was projected on the walls, while spoken word echoed around you, creating a living work of art that changed over time. Jules Gimbrone has used a series of glass vessels filled with liquids to explore how sound recordings echo and amplify in the small space. There have also been giant rock formations embedded with hundreds of tiny black-and-white photos. You have to figure out what makes each piece a sculpture. That's half the challenge.

Address 44-19 Purves Street, Long Island City, NY 11101, +1 (718)361-1750, www.sculpture-center.org, info@sculpture-center.org | Getting there Subway to Queens Plaza (E, M, R), Court Square (7) | Hours Thu–Mon 11am–6pm | Tip Defy gravity at the massively colorful Cliffs at LIC. This indoor climbing gym is enormous, and you'll tackle 60-foot-high walls. They also offer ladies-only bouldering classes (11-11 44th Drive, Long Island City, NY 11101, www.lic.thecliffsclimbing.com).

# 97 — Self-Taught Genius Gallery

*Go inside for the outsider art*

Among the parked semi-trucks and large loading docks is a hidden museum, where the self-taught artist is celebrated. Ring the bell, and they will buzz you into this industrial warehouse. Take the stairway to the second floor, and you've walked into a creative world unlike any other. The single room is filled with drawings, handmade books, animal sculptures, furniture, paintings, ceramics, and watercolors. It's a curious collection, all made by artists with no formal training, but who look to life experience instead.

These works are gems from the permanent collection of the American Folk Art Museum. The museum shows thematic exhibitions at their Lincoln Center location, but this gallery is where the collection's best of the best is on view. Iconic pieces are taken out of storage and made visible for all.

You'll often see works by Ammi Phillips (1788–1865), the itinerant American portrait painter, whose bold, flat planes of color create compelling images of 19th-century subjects. The quiet poses are striking in their own way. But you may also see pieces by one of America's most celebrated outsider artists, Henry Darger (1892–1973), who worked as a janitor in a Chicago hospital. He became famous only after he died, when a lifetime of elaborately painted manuscripts were discovered. Large, scroll-like paintings show fantastical children and creatures romping through the forest and fighting wars. They are both bucolic and terrifying as one man's private obsession.

Also look for rotating textile masterpieces from the museum's stellar quilt collection. Soldier's quilts were stitched by men convalescing in military hospitals. The 19th-century designs were made from military uniforms and were brightly geometric. By contrast, elegant white-on-white quilts have the most delicate stitching.

**Address** 47-29 32nd Place, Long Island City, NY 11101, +1 (212)595-9533, www.folkartmuseum.org, info@folkartmuseum.org | **Getting there** Subway to 33rd Street (7); bus to Queens Boulevard/35th Street (Q32), 48th Avenue/33rd Street (Q39), Queens Boulevard/35th Street (Q60) | **Hours** Mon–Thu 11am–5pm | **Tip** Head over to the Hudson River Greenway, where dramatic stone sculptures often line the bank; the ephemeral formations are by artist Uliks Gryka, who is a master at balance and assembly (Sisyphus Stones; Hudson River Greenway in Fort Washington Park, south of George Washington Bridge).

# 98 The Skyscraper Museum
*A tall tale of reaching for the heights*

Just like the pencil thin, super slender high-rises that are springing up all over New York City, the Skyscraper Museum in Battery Park City is a sliver of a space that aims high. But what it lacks in size, it makes up for in spirit, offering big insights into the world's first vertical metropolis that is Manhattan. It's been a fascinating climb.

You'll find photos, models, and memorabilia chronicling the human pursuit to build ever higher, and the stories of architectural and engineering feats that made builders reach for the sky. The rise of One World Trade Center takes center stage here, with a working model of the building's spire. The building was designed to be 1,776 feet high, a symbolic number associated with American Independence. The final design shifted over time, and in a duel with the Sears/Willis Tower of Chicago, One World Trade was designated the tallest building in North America. It all came down to its striking spire, which was deemed part of the structure.

Don't miss the wooden models of Manhattan. Painstakingly carved by Arizona amateur model maker Michael G. Chesko, each tiny building is sized to perfect scale. Using online data and satellite imagery, Chesko recreated Midtown and Lower Manhattan as doll-sized edifices. He donated the models to the museum, and in 2000, he drove across the country to transport the pint-sized panoramas. It was actually his first trip to Manhattan and a chance to see the real city at scale.

The museum also offers a special web project that chronicles New York City's Super-Slenders, the thin skyscrapers that are quickly becoming so common all over Manhattan. These ultra-luxury towers soar up to 90 stories high, and their slender proportions are calculated by the width of the base to the height of the structure. They represent a new challenge in the ever-competitive race to create edgy architectural design.

Address 39 Battery Place, New York, NY 10280, +1 (212)968-1961, www.skyscraper.org, info@skyscraper.org | Getting there Subway to Bowling Green (4, 5), Rector Street (1, R, W) | Hours Wed – Sun noon – 6pm | Tip For the ultimate high rise, go to the new World Trade Center Tower and take the elevator up 100 floors to One World Observatory for panoramic views of Manhattan and beyond. The elevator rides up and down are actually quite exhilarating – you'll see why (285 Fulton Street, entrance on West Street, New York, NY 10007, www.oneworldobservatory.com).

# 99__Society of Illustrators

*Staying outside the lines*

With our daily deluge of social media photos, its nice to know the fine art of drawing by hand is alive and well. The Society of Illustrators on the Upper East Side, housed in a stately townhouse on a tawny street, is a hidden temple of illustration. An old boy's club when it opened in 1901, the society was where distinguished illustrators gathered to dine, draw, and discuss. It's very modern now and open to everyone.

"People do not realize what incredible art they are going to see throughout the building, even in the bathrooms," says executive director Anelle Miller. On some evenings you'll see a cache of people sitting around a makeshift stage while nude or curiously costumed models hold long poses. Welcome to the beloved Sketch Night, where amateurs and professionals sit side by side, drawing from life. Sultry jazz music inspires. Cocktails refresh. Now that's what you call a fine evening.

Don't miss the second-floor staircase, where you'll see dozens of portrait sketches of past presidents. Finely detailed or spare and simple, they are a sampling of sketching styles over the years. In the Hall of Fame Dining Room on the third floor is the Society's welcoming bar. With floor-to-ceiling windows, it's one of the city's best-kept secrets. Above the bar hangs Norman Rockwell's colorful painting, *The Dover Coach*, which he gifted to the Society in 1939.

The Society hosts rotating exhibitions of the graphic arts, from Spider Man to fashion illustration, cartoons to computer-generated imagery. You forget how varied and entertaining illustrations can be. They are a bit easier to digest than thickly layered oil paintings. The hand-drawn image feels immediate, a direct connection to the artist. Ponder that idea over a lunch in the Society's retro-feeling 128 Bar & Bistro. With its brick walls and charming terrace, it's the quintessential Upper East Side haunt.

Address 128 East 63rd Street, New York, NY 10065, +1 (212)838-2560,
www.societyillustrators.org, info@societyillustrators.org | Getting there Subway to
Lexington Avenue/63rd Street (F, N, Q), or Lexington Avenue/59th Street (4, 5, 6) |
Hours Tue & Thu 10am–8pm, Wed & Fri 10am–5pm, Sat 11am–5pm | Tip Visit the
quaint, European eatery Bel Ami Café. It's perfect for a quick salad or sandwich (30 East
68th Street, New York, NY 10065, www.belamicafeny.com).

# 100 The Solomon R. Guggenheim

*Art in the round*

Amidst the ornate Beaux Arts buildings on the Upper East Side, the 1959 Guggenheim museum is a bit of a shock, as if a spaceship had touched down on 89th Street. Architect Frank Lloyd Wright wanted to design a modern building for modern art. To say that he achieved his goal would be an understatement.

Pass through the front door, and it feels a bit cramped. However, a shallow doorway is, by design, delivering you into a soaring, cathedral-like rotunda, one of the many ways Wright shaped the space to guide you along. The architect never cared for New York City but loved nature. So he added broad windows overlooking Central Park and repeated those organic shapes inside.

Begin your climb up the multiple ramps circling the rotunda. All the way at the top, a glorious, glass oculus crowns the space. Exhibitions rotate and feature modern and contemporary art. Works from the permanent collection are found in the Thannhauser Gallery. Paintings by Cézanne, Gauguin, and Manet are often on view, along with the iconic *Woman Ironing* by Pablo Picasso. Rendered in blues and grays, the angular woman presses a hot iron into the wrinkled fabric. She appears melancholy and gaunt, one of the working poor Picasso captured during his Blue Period in Paris.

Then step back on the ramp and continue your climb. Art works are visible across the rotunda, below, and above. It's an immersive, 360-degree experience, where you are part of a community made up of everyone in the museum. Wright was actually criticized early on. Some thought the building was competing with the art. He disagreed, responding confidently, "on the contrary, it was to make the building and the painting a beautiful symphony such as never existed in the world of art before."

Address 1071 5th Avenue, New York, NY 10128, +1 (212)423-3500, www.guggenheim.org, visitorinfo@guggenheim.org | Getting there Subway to 86th Street (4, 5, 6, Q) | Hours Mon–Wed, Fri & Sun 10am–5:45pm, Sat 10am–7:45pm | Tip Take a walk around the iconic Jacqueline Kennedy Onassis Reservoir across the street in Central Park (enter on 86th Street at 5th Avenue, www.centralpark.com/things-to-do/attractions/reservoir).

THE SOLOMON R GUGGENHEIM MUSEUM

# 101— South Street Seaport Museum

*For the love of ships*

You first notice the cobblestone streats. Then, the perfectly preserved little storefronts that bring us back to the history of the Seaport District NYC. Bustling with trade, this was the 'it' neighborhood in the early 1800s. Ships from all over the world docked at the nearby piers and brought coffee, tea, and other precious cargo to the New World.

Dive into that milieu at the South Street Seaport Museum, which specializes in the seafaring life of New York City. Learn about the transatlantic cruise ships in the era of the *Titanic*, and the different experiences between traveling in first class and in steerage class. You can see actual 1906 dining menus, plates, cups, and flatware from the SS *Arabic*, where the world's wealthy travelers were offered sirloin of beef, lamb with mint sauce, and apple charlotte. Dining fare in third class was far more perfunctory, with gruel along with grilled sausages and stewed peaches.

In the early 1900s, nearly 13 million immigrants traveled to America on board these vessels. Crammed into bunk beds on the lower levels, they had little space. Above, luxury travelers enjoyed a palm garden, writing room, Turkish bath, and even a department store. You can actually feel a piece of first-class grandeur with a recreated wood panel from the RMS *Mauretania* smoking room. Very luxurious indeed.

Then take a stroll along the museum's famed Street of Ships, where the historic waterfront comes to life. Five sailing vessels are docked here. Especially popular is the 1907 *Ambrose*, a floating lighthouse that helped safely guide ships into the New York harbor. Then go on board the 1885 *Wavertree*, which the city spent 13 million dollars to restore. It was one of the last large sailing ships built of wrought iron, and it is the literal flagship of the museum.

**Address** 12 Fulton Street, New York, NY 10038, +1 (212)748-8600, www.southstreetseaportmuseum.org | **Getting there** Subway to Fulton Street (A, C, J, Z, 2, 3, 4, 5) | **Hours** Wed–Sun 11am–5pm | **Tip** Avoid the crowds near Times Square, and snap up discount Broadway show tickets at the far more relaxed TKTS location in the Seaport (190 Front Street, New York, NY 10038, www.tdf.org).

# 102 Spyscape

*What kind of spy are you?*

Grab your trench coat and black fedora, and head over to New York's entertaining spy museum, where your covert abilities are tested in secret code. With the design elements of a trendy hotel lobby or chic nightclub, this new breed of museum turns discovery into an immersive experience. When you leave, you'll know if you're the next James Bond.

Upon arrival, you receive a tricked-out wristband that allows you to access the exhibits. And then you are escorted onto the gigantic briefing elevator with 3-D videos. It will orient you into this secret world. Step outside, where black walls, polished concrete floors, and silver pools of light feel like a minimalistic 007 loft. Throughout these galleries, techno stations test your brainpower while collecting your personal data along the way. Ready, set, go.

First off, have a seat inside the lie-detection booth to see if you can spot the liar – and whether you're a good liar yourself. (Tip: Don't touch your face or blink too much.) Next, step into the Special Ops Laser Tunnel, where your agility is put to the test. You try to hit a series of spot-lit targets while avoiding the web of green laser lights above and below. It's a game of high-tech Twister meets yoga. Then you are quizzed on your ability to take chances, or your skill at decoding encryption. And finally, the surveillance video gallery tests your eye for observing small details of human interaction. The man to the left on screen 34 – was his shirt red or orange?

You'll also get mini tutorials about real-life famous spies, like Joan Clarke and Alan Turing, who cracked the German Enigma Code during World War ll. Finally, head to the Debriefing Room to check out your own data. A computer will tell you what kind of spy you might be: Intelligence Operative, Spycatcher, or Cryptologist. Then in seconds, the screen dissolves before your eyes. Mission accomplished.

Address 928 8th Avenue, New York, NY 10019, +1 (212)549-1941, www.spyscape.com |
Getting there Subway to 50th Street (C, E), 59th Street Columbus Circle (A, B, C, D),
57th Street (N, Q, R) | Hours Mon–Fri 10am–9pm, Sat & Sun 9am–9pm | Tip The
nearby Hearst Tower blends old and new with a modern glass high rise built on top of
an historic art deco building (959 8th Avenue, New York, NY 10019, www.hearst.com/
real-estate/hearst-tower).

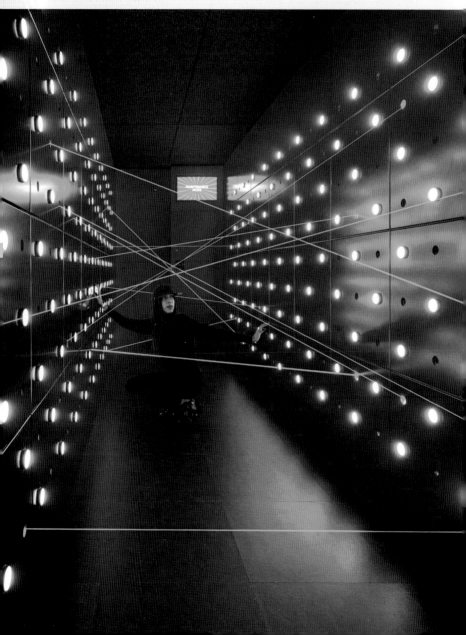

# 103 Staten Island Museum

*A wonderland of discovery*

The soaring, colossal columns at the entrance to the Staten Island Museum make for a most impressive welcome. The museum is housed in an 1874 former dormitory for retired sailors. The fully renovated building has Victorian-era bones mixed with modern-day flair. It's sometimes thought of as a mini Smithsonian because of its great variety of collections. Clearly, there's something here for everyone.

Begin with the museum's mascot, the giant Mastodon. He's not real, but a pretty convincing replica bursts out of the wall. This massive animal with the tremendous tusks is now extinct, but the story here is about preservation of today's species. We see an actual Mastodon molar, nearly the size of a football. It is proof that the wooly beasts once roamed this area.

Curiosities from all over the world are found in the "Opening the Treasure Box" exhibit, with fascinating objects spanning 5,000 years. The oldest is an ancient Egyptian funerary statuette of a striding man. Also on view, an intricately embroidered dragon robe from Imperial China. In other galleries you'll find rich and varied art offerings, like a collection of landscape paintings showing views of the island's edge. It's a nice, varied tour through the different spaces here, with a great sense of discovery.

Conveniently, the museum is situated right in the middle of the Snug Harbor Cultural Center, an 83-acre park with graceful Greek Revival buildings. It's a Staten Island wonderland. You can explore tales of the sea at the nearby Noble Maritime Collection. Or sample botanic beauties at the Chinese Scholar's Garden, with its many pavilions and waterfall. The Tuscan Garden is modeled after the Villa Gamberaia in Florence. There is even a secret medieval garden, where you can get lost in a complex maze of hedges. It's as if you've traveled far away, and yet you never had to leave New York City.

Address 1000 Richmond Terrace, Building A, Staten Island, NY 10301, +1 (718)727-1135, www.statenislandmuseum.org, info@statenislandmuseum.org | Getting there Staten Island Ferry, then bus S 40 to Snug Harbor | Hours Wed–Sun 11am–5pm | Tip From paintings to sculptures, the Newhouse Center for Contemporary Art offers a variety of exhibitions featuring experimental art from around the world (Buildings C and G, www.snug-harbor.org/visual-arts/newhouse-center-for-contemporary-art).

# 104__ Tenement Museum
*How new Americans lived*

Only in New York City could a run-down tenement be turned into one of the most beloved museums in the city. That's the story of the Lower East Side's Tenement Museum, where tales of the American immigrant are brought to life in vivid detail. Multiple family tenement buildings were the first American homes for thousands of immigrants. Through guided visits, the museum teaches history through the lives of actual families who lived here and their heartbreaking struggles to survive. Step into the narrow entryway, and a time capsule awaits you – with peeling paint, rippled floors, and burlap-clad walls. The space is purposely left raw to show the toll these buildings endured over time. Upstairs, we see how families lived, starting with the German-Jewish Gumpertz family in the 325-square-foot apartment.

The six members of the Gumpertz family lived in these three dark rooms. During cold nights, they slept beside the stove. There was no running water. The entire building shared an uncomfortable outdoor toilet. In the economic Panic of 1873, the father disappeared, leaving Mrs. Gumpertz alone with their four small children. In the tiny front room, we see a sewing machine, which Mrs. Gumpertz eventually used to earn money as a dressmaker.

Another story comes to life in the 1928 apartment of the Italian Baldizzi family, who lived there through the Great Depression. We can picture family gatherings in this small apartment with a coal stove and a cheery red floral tablecloth. Through recorded voice, we actually hear Josephine Baldizzi Esposito recall her life here as a little girl. Now a grandmother in Brooklyn, she shares the simple Saturday treat of scrambled eggs served with ketchup while listening to Italian opera. Her colorful voice makes the tiny kitchen come alive, a poignant connection to the immigrant story that stays with you long after the visit is over.

Address 103 Orchard Street, New York, NY 10002, +1 (877)975-3786, www.tenement.org, lestm@tenement.org | Getting there Subway to Grand Street (B, D), Delancey Street (F), Essex Street (J, M, Z) | Hours Guided tours only; see website for tour topics and times | Tip Visit the Essex Street Market, one of the city's most historic institutions. Mayor LaGuardia built it in the 1940s to get throngs of pushcarts off the streets and make way for cars. Today it is filled with food vendors selling produce, proteins, and baked goods of all kinds (120 Essex Street, New York, NY 10002, www.essexstreetmarket.com).

# 105 — Theodore Roosevelt Birthplace National Historic Site

*A boy with a mission*

With his reputation as a robust adventurer, America's 26th president, Theodore Roosevelt was actually a sickly child. You can tour the family's striking brownstone, which has lush wallpapers and twinkling chandeliers. Born here in 1858, Roosevelt had a childhood that was one of affluence, but within that elegant house, young Roosevelt suffered from asthma attacks that kept him out of school. 'Teedie,' as he was called, considered the family library gloomy, but he found comfort in adventure books. You can see the gas lamps he read by, along with his special childhood red reading chair.

The townhouse itself boasts stained-glass doors, carved tables, and porcelain plates, an incongruous setting for young Roosevelt's obsession with animals. He kept live snakes in the kitchen and trays of dead mice in the ice box. The smell of arsenic would waft throughout the opulent rooms, as the boy practiced taxidermy. But his body was failing. Just off the nursery is a covered porch where Roosevelt began exercising to build his strength. Imagine the young boy dreaming of a big life.

His life turned out very big, and many personal artifacts are on view here, including campaign buttons, uniforms, and diaries. The most arresting display is a white shirt hanging in a vitrine. In 1912, Roosevelt was getting ready to give a speech in Milwaukee, when he was shot by an assailant. The bullet lodged in his chest, just short of his lung. But most of the force was absorbed by a metal glasses case in his pocket, along with a folded, 50-page speech. He gave the talk anyway and was treated only afterwards. The glasses case and the speech are in this museum, along with the white shirt with the bullet hole. This historic house offers fascinating insights into this charismatic man.

Address 28 East 20th Street, New York, NY 10003, +1 (212)260-1616, www.nps.gov/thrb |
Getting there Subway to Union Square/14th Street (4,5, L, N, Q), 23rd Street (6),
23rd Street (R) | Hours Tue – Sat 9am – 5pm | Tip For more old-world elegance, take a
stroll around the nearby Gramercy Park and peek through the locked gates. Only lucky
neighborhood residents have keys to get into this private oasis (Lexington Avenue at
21st Street, New York, NY 10010).

# 106__THNK 1994 Museum
*Irresistible DIY pop culture*

Who says you can't open up your own museum right in the hallway of your small, Brooklyn apartment? That's how the irreverent THNK 1994 Museum came to be the brainchild of roommates and museum co-founders Matt Harkins and Viviana Rosales Olen. It all started in 2015, when the two comedians were watching a documentary about infamous Olympic skaters Tonya Harding and Nancy Kerrigan. Naming the museum after the skater's initials (TH and NK), they started a Kickstarter campaign to raise $75. They received more than $2,000, along with donations of art and artifacts. For two years, visitors from all over the world came to see the gallery in their 25-foot-long hallway filled with Tonya and Nancy photos, artwork, and videos.

They moved the museum out of their apartment and into a gallery in Brooklyn. "Right here we have selections from our permanent collection," Viviana says. "These were lovingly made and donated to the museum from people all over the country." There's a pair of needlepoint portraits of Tonya and Nancy, a Tonya diorama, and tiny figurines of both skaters set inside jeweled frames. "This is really the genesis of our collection," Matt says dryly.

Recently, they've expanded the focus. There have been exhibits on the Olsen Twins, along with an exhibition on Kim Cattrall of *Sex and the City* – "because she is so fabulous," Viviana coos. The exhibit "Celebrities Smoking in the Bathroom at the Met Gala" was quite well received.

"We're 100 percent dedicated to this as a lifestyle," Matt explains. They now work on the museum full-time. A DIY work in progress, it's a museum, turned pop-up, turned pop culture hang out. Half the fun is following along to see where they will show up next. Don't miss the hilarious video on their website, where Matt and Viviana give a tour of the original THNK 1994 Museum in their original apartment hallway.

**Address** 1436 Atlantic Avenue, Brooklyn, NY 11216, +1 (347)334-0946, www.thnk1994.com, info@thnk1994.com | **Getting there** Subway to Kingston/Throop Avenues (C), Nostrand Avenue (A), Kingston Avenue (3) | **Hours** See the website for their current pop-up location, along with exhibition dates and times | **Tip** Let your inner Tonya or Nancy shine at the Lefrak Center's roller-skating (Apr–Oct) or ice-skating (Nov–Mar) rink at Lakeside in Prospect Park (171 East Drive, Brooklyn, NY 11225, www.lakesidebrooklyn.com).

# 107 Ukrainian Institute

*Inside a Museum Mile mansion*

The Ukrainian Institute is an impossibly ornate, neo-French-Gothic mansion at the corner of 79th Street and Fifth Avenue. But don't just walk past. You can actually go inside this limestone landmark, one of the city's best hidden treasures. Look up and you'll see tiny turrets with cross-shaped finials accenting the building's top while scowling dragons keep watch. Don't miss the little munchkins flanking the front doorway. They seem eerily alive.

Also known as the Fletcher-Sinclair mansion, this was a private residence built in 1899 by architect C.P.H. Gilbert. After a series of owners, it became home to the Ukrainian Institute in 1955. It's only partially furnished, so the bones of the building can really shine. Concerts, lectures, and art exhibitions are held here in great fashion. The crowning treat is the tiny museum on the top floor, which is like a visit to the private art collection of an urbane friend.

Make your way up the wood-carved, central stairway, where a very royal looking chandelier dangles from above. There's an oval-shaped sitting room and a charming, glassed-in corner turret, which magically hovers over 79th Street. It feels as if someone just abandoned this regal residence, and you have it to yourself.

The visual joys culminate on the top floor where the works of Ukrainian artist Alexander Archipenko (1887–1964) come alive. Like Picasso in the early 1900s, Archipenko worked in the cubist style and later turned to more simplified forms. An abstract painting in gouache breaks a guitar down to faceted planes. A bronze sculpture of a woman, head resting on knee, looks quietly serene. The selected works are from the collection of Augustin and Maria Sumyk and are on long-term view in this airy space.

One by one, the works offer a fresh look at modernism, and discovering them inside this Gilded Age mansion is quintessential New York.

Address 2 East 79th Street, New York, NY 10075, +1 (212)288-8660, www.ukrainianinstitute.org, mail@ukrainianinstitute.org | Getting there Subway to 77th Street (6), 86th Street (4, 5, 6) | Hours Tue–Sat noon–6pm | Tip For a superb Italian coffee and great gelato, stop by Sant Ambroeus (1000 Madison Avenue, New York, NY 10021, www.santambroeus.com).

# 108 United Nations Art Collection

*A world of art*

The United Nations headquarters is a soaring slab of a skyscraper that perfectly embodies the International Style of architecture: bold, assertive, and unapologetically modern. But what many people don't know is that it houses one of the finest art collections in the city. And it's open to the public free of charge.

Find your way past security to the outdoor courtyard situated along the East River. Here the impressive *Non-Violence* bronze gun sculpture takes place of honor. This oversized .357 Magnum revolver, with a knotted muzzle aiming upwards, is by Swedish artist Carl Reuterswärd. This powerful sculpture was made in 1985 after the murder of his friend John Lennon. Located nearby is *Sphere Within Sphere*, completed in 1993 by Italian artist Arnaldo Pomodoro. One of many versions around the world, it is a reflective poem about the earth's fragility. Most of the works are gifts by UN member nations and meet the rigorous standards of the UN Art Committee. They have themes of peace, humanity, and wonder and are poignant sentiments that highlight the UN's great mission.

You sense that mission as you enter the soaring, light-filled lobby, where mere humans are dwarfed in scale. Suspended above is a replica of the Soviet Sputnik, the world's first satellite and a thrilling gift from the then Soviet Union. So too is the cobalt blue stained-glass window by Marc Chagall. This 15-foot-long masterpiece commemorates former UN Secretary General Dag Hammarskjöld and represents a place of quiet contemplation.

If you take a tour, you'll get to see the *Golden Rule* mosaic based on a Norman Rockwell painting. A gift of Nancy Reagan in 1985, it depicts people of all races and is an ode to humanity and peace. The art inside this iconic space is as inspiring as the UN's own mission.

Address 405 East 42nd Street, New York, NY 10017 (enter Visitor Centre at 46th Street & 1st Avenue), +1 (212)963-4475, www.visitun.org | Getting there Subway to Grand Central/42nd Street (4, 5, 6, 7), Lexington Avenue/53rd Street (E, M) | Hours Mon–Fri 9am–4:45pm | Tip With stunning views of the East River, have lunch in exquisite Mad Men splendor at the UN Delegates Dining Room (ddr-reservations.com).

# 109__Waterfront Museum

*Dropping anchor in Brooklyn*

It's all about the waterfront in Brooklyn's Dumbo neighborhood. And right in the trendy center of it all, the Brooklyn Historical Society has opened a little storefront museum called Waterfront. The museum is housed inside Empire Stores, a Civil War-era warehouse turned retail space. Here you can grab a coffee, buy a leather satchel, and wander into the little Waterfront museum all in one stop. It's history where people like to hang out.

The museum is airy and modern. Large glass windows offer glimpses of the East River right outside your door. Set up like a boutique, there are free-standing stations that explore the many lives of the Brooklyn waterfront and its future. Visitors can spend a few minutes or an hour as there are quick bites of history for all ages.

Start with the ground beneath your feet. Little pull-out drawers show you archaeological artifacts actually found in the landfill underneath the warehouse. A drawer labeled *Smoking on the Job* reveals clay pipe fragments and tells visitors how smoking tobacco was a part of daily life in 19th-century Brooklyn. Another drawer displays a cow bone, perhaps discarded by a local butcher. You can put your nose to the test exploring the kinds of goods once stored inside this warehouse. Little pull-out bins offer smells of coffee, sugar, and tobacco. Sensory immersion for sure.

The lives of women play a big role, and you can hear stories from a female welder who worked at the Brooklyn Navy Yard. Colorful graffiti panels show the 20th-century influx of artists to the waterfront, which helped Dumbo flourish as a tech and tourist hotspot. Finally, there's always an eye to the future. An interactive exhibition looks to climate change and the possible challenges of rising water in the decades ahead. Past, present, and future, it's the iconic Brooklyn waterfront at your fingertips.

Address 55 Water Street (Brooklyn Bridge Park), Brooklyn, NY 11201, +1 (718)222-4111, www.brooklynhistory.org | Getting there Subway to High Street (A, C), Clark Street (2, 3), York Street (F) | Hours Tue–Thu, Sun 11am–6pm, Fri & Sat 11am–8pm | Tip Hop on and off the NYC Ferry for a waterside tour of New York City. Six routes offer unique views of the Big Apple (Old Fulton Street/Furman Street, Brooklyn, NY 11201, www.ferry.nyc/routes-and-schedules).

# 110__The Whitney Museum
*A hot spot for art*

What a difference a new building can make. With its cantilevered entrance, glassed-in lobby, and shimmering views of the Hudson River, the new Whitney Museum has become the gathering place in the Meatpacking District. Designed in 2015 by architect Renzo Piano, outdoor terraces hover over the High Line walking paths, connecting art and everyday life.

Inside, the feel is modern-industrial with its pine floors, broad windows, and expansive galleries. The focus here is on American art with 20th-century and contemporary offerings. And with a permanent collection of some 23,000 works, the holdings are deep. There has always been a special focus on living American artists, and stalwarts like Cy Twombly, Jasper Johns, and Cindy Sherman had their first museum retrospectives at the Whitney. Even today, curators seek out artists before they are well known, often purchasing works the very year they are created.

It's a mission that goes back to 1931, when the museum was first opened by wealthy socialite and art patron Gertrude Vanderbilt Whitney. A sculptor herself, Whitney purchased works by early 20th-century American artists who were exploring new ideas. Paintings by George Bellows, Edward Hopper, and Stuart Davis were part of the early collection. In 1929, Whitney offered to donate several hundred works to the Metropolitan Museum of Art. When they declined the gift, she decided to open her own museum (see ch. 111).

That spirit of discovery remains the focus today. Exhibitions rotate and might feature a single artist, theme, or period of time. But it's the museum's legendary Whitney Biennial that packs the biggest art-world punch. Started in 1973, curators seek out little-known or emerging artists and show their works side by side throughout the museum. It's powerful recognition that in the past helped bring artists like Jackson Pollock and Jeff Koons to prominence.

Address 99 Gansevoort Street, New York, NY 10014, +1 (212)570-3600, www.whitney.org, info@whitney.org | Getting there Subway to 14th Street (A, C, E, L) | Hours Mon, Wed, Thu, Sun 10:30am–6pm, Fri & Sat 10:30am–10pm | Tip Art and nature converge with a walk on the High Line. The elevated walking path features dozens of site-specific sculptures and installations that are cool and cutting edge (enter at Gansevoort & Washington Streets, New York, NY 10014, www.art.thehighline.org).

# 111 The Whitney Studio

*An atelier in an alley*

If only more people had listened to sculptor Gertrude Vanderbilt Whitney back in the 1920s. While most New Yorkers were still swooning over European art, she was championing fellow American artists breaking new ground, including Edward Hopper and Stuart Davis. She showed and purchased this new kind of art for years. In 1929, when she offered several hundred pieces to the Metropolitan Museum of Art, they said, "No, thank you." Undeterred, she started her own museum, which is now the iconic Whitney Museum of American Art in New York City (see ch. 110). So it all worked out fine for everyone, especially us.

Explore the early days of American art with a private tour of Vanderbilt Whitney's dreamy atelier, hidden away along MacDougal Alley in Greenwich Village. It's housed in the very building where she first opened her museum in 1931, now home to the New York Studio School.

The alley was built for horses, not wealthy Vanderbilts, when she moved into the former hayloft in 1907. Warm light embraces in the small studio, which hovers over the alley. And anchoring the entire space is an enormous, 20-foot-tall fireplace, designed by Robert Winthrop Chanler. Twisting and writhing plaster flames cover the surface, as if the entire chimneypiece were on fire. It pushes up to the plaster ceiling, where curious winged dragons and demons swirl, all formed in low relief. And even though today the studio is all white, in its time, Vanderbilt Whitney had the dramatic fireplace painted bright red, green, and gold polychrome.

See other studios here too, with skylights above and aged floorboards below. Today they are filled with sculptors at work, all hailing from the art school. It's an atmospheric look back in time, to when the stirrings of modern American art were filling this hidden alleyway, preserved here today because of one woman's singular vision.

Address 8 West 8th Street, New York, NY 10011, +1 (212)673-6466, www.nyss.org, info@nyss.org | Getting there Subway to West 4th Street-Washington Square (A, B, C, D, E, F, M), 8th Street Station (R, W) | Hours Private tours only, call to arrange | Tip Revel in the bohemian spirit of today's New York in Washington Square Park, where flowers are blooming and musicians are often playing, sometimes on a grand piano (West 4th Street & Macdougal Street, New York, NY 10011).

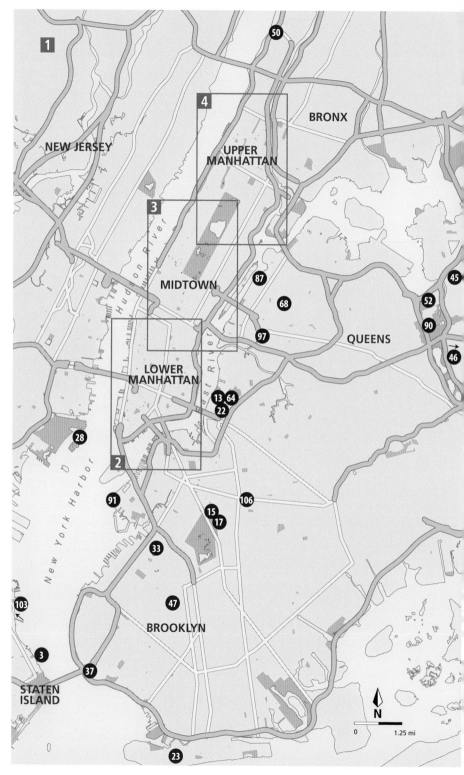

John Major, Ed Lefkowicz
**111 Places in Brooklyn**
**That You Must Not Miss**
ISBN 978-3-7408-0380-3

Anita Mai Genua,
Clare Davenport,
Elizabeth Lenell Davies
**111 Places in Toronto**
**That You Must Not Miss**
ISBN 978-3-7408-0257-8

Andréa Seiger
**111 Places in Washington D.C.**
**That You Must Not Miss**
ISBN 978-3-7408-0258-5

Elisabeth Larsen
**111 Places in The Twin Cities**
**That You Must Not Miss**
ISBN 978-3-7408-0029-1

Joe DiStefano, Clay Williams
**111 Places in Queens**
**That You Must Not Miss**
ISBN 978-3-7408-0020-8

Allison Robicelli, John Dean
**111 Places in Baltimore**
**That You Must Not Miss**
ISBN 978-3-7408-0158-8

Amy Bizzarri, Susie Inverso
**111 Places in Chicago**
**That You Must Not Miss**
ISBN 978-3-7408-0156-4

Laurel Moglen, Julia Posey,
Lyudmila Zotova
**111 Places in Los Angeles**
**That You Must Not Miss**
ISBN 978-3-95451-884-5

Gordon Streisand
**111 Places in Miami and the**
**Keys That You Must Not Miss**
ISBN 978-3-95451-644-5

Floriana Petersen,
Steve Werney
**111 Places in San Francisco
That You Must Not Miss**
ISBN 978-3-95451-609-4

Jo-Anne Elikann
**111 Places in New York
That You Must Not Miss**
ISBN 978-3-95451-052-8

Michael Murphy, Sally Asher
**111 Places in New Orleans
That You Must Not Miss**
ISBN 978-3-95451-645-2

Tom Shields, Gillian Tait
**111 Places in Glasgow
That You Shouldn't Miss**
ISBN 978-3-7408-0256-1

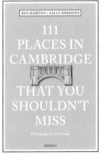

Rosalind Horton,
Sally Simmons, Guy Snape
**111 Places in Cambridge
That You Shouldn't Miss**
ISBN 978-3-7408-0147-2

Justin Postlethwaite
**111 Places in Bath
That You Shouldn't Miss**
ISBN 978-3-7408-0146-5

Gillian Tait
**111 Places in Edinburgh
That You Shouldn't Miss**
ISBN 978-3-95451-883-8

Julian Treuherz,
Peter de Figueiredo
**111 Places in Liverpool
That You Shouldn't Miss**
ISBN 978-3-95451-769-5

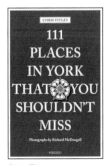

Chris Titley
**111 Places in York
That You Shouldn't Miss**
ISBN 978-3-95451-768-8

## Acknowledgements

Thank you to my publisher and the team at Emons Verlag for creating a book about museums. To my editor Karen Seiger, thank you for your cheerfulness and patience. Thank you to Ed Lefkowicz for your inspiring images. And thank you to Laura Olk, for putting the pieces together. And I am grateful for a chance meeting with John Brancati, where the idea for this book was hatched.
– Wendy Lubovich

My most profuse thanks to my wife Cynthia Lefkowicz for her patience, forbearance, help, and encouragement throughout this project, and for suggesting and orchestrating our move from New England to New York nearly 8 years ago. New York's many museums were a major draw for us both. And if cities are where ideas go to have sex, this city is arguably the most fertile. To Karen Seiger I owe much for bringing me into this project, and to Wendy Lubovich for her words and insight. Finally, thanks to the memory of my father Constanty Lefkowicz, who first introduced me to the magic of photography.
– Ed Lefkowicz

*The author*

**Wendy Lubovich** is a museum buff extraordinaire. As a private guide in New York City, she takes clients from around the world to museums big and small. With a Fine and Decorative Arts degree from Christie's Education in London, she understands the nuance of the art world. And as an experienced journalist, she's developed a keen sense of curiosity. Her passion is to connect people and museums in a creative and conversational way, inspiring a sense of wonder and fun.

*The photographer*

**Ed Lefkowicz** is a commercial, corporate, and editorial photographer. A native New Englander who eventually moved to Brooklyn with his wife Cynthia, he enjoys exploring New York City life in all its storied quirkiness. Never without a camera, he chronicles the cognitive dissonances that color life in the boroughs with his alt website TheQuirkySide.com. As photo editor of *Edible Queens* magazine, he fancies himself a *saveur* and may have been the first to introduce the American term 'foodie' to the French.